WHY THE JAPANESE
HAVE BEEN
SO SUCCESSFUL
IN BUSINESS

WHY THE JAPANESE HAVE BEEN SO SUCCESSFUL IN BUSINESS

by

Friedrich Fürstenberg
with commentary on the English translation
by George Copeman

LEVIATHAN HOUSE
LONDON
HIPPOCRENE BOOKS
NEW YORK

First published in English 1974
© Copyright Leviathan House Ltd 1974
First published in German by Verlag Moderne Industrie A G,
Zurich, 1972

ISBN 0 900537 11 6

Library of Congress Catalog Card No
    73-77702

Distributed in the United States by Hippocrene Books Inc.,
171 Madison Avenue, New York, N.Y. 10016.

Printed in Great Britain
By W & J Mackay Limited, Chatham

Contents

Foreword

by
C. Northcote Parkinson

Consideration of the phenomenal rise of Japanese industry, especially since World War II, has led many business men to ask what the secret is of Japanese success. Will it continue? And have the Japanese some techniques which we could imitate? These questions have now been answered by Friedrich Fürstenberg. As Germany too can claim to have staged an economic miracle, a German author is well placed to study the Japanese achievement. He has done so with German thoroughness, producing a masterly analysis of all that is peculiar to Japanese industry. His work will be of the greatest interest to every manager, of the highest value to every student of modern industry. We ignore this book at our peril, remembering that the Far East is a region of growing importance. There are some significant lessons to be learnt and Dr. George Copeman has summarised them at the end for the benefit of British and American readers.

All industrial countries have been at one time agricultural. Where the Japanese are most remarkable is in the speed with which they have industrialised their country, mostly since World War II. The author of this book gives us the startling fact that 40·5% of the workers in Japan were still agricultural in 1955, the proportion falling to 18·8% by 1969. This represents a revolutionary rate of change. As against that, the change itself follows a normal pattern. In every agricultural country the peasant works with a conscience. His task is something that has to be done. Beasts must be fed and cows must be milked, fields must be dug and plants must be watered. Within the limits set by season and weather, the work is something on which life depends. If crops and animals die, the men die too. It is probable that the peasant also derives extra energy from the freshness of his food supply, the mettle of his pasture. When supplanted by agricultural machinery and brought into the factory, the peasant works as he did on the land, applying his energy and conscience to a task that is no longer interrupted by the weather. His son will do the same from his schooldays onward and so will his grandson, but the impetus will be gradually lost, partly perhaps because of changes in diet and partly because the work is no longer vital. To maintain a certain level of production may be desirable, as the foreman will explain, but it is not a condition of survival. To down tools may be thought a serious matter but it is no longer a form of suicide. In the peasant's great-grandson conscience is no longer the guiding motive. Other ideas may well predominate. We can trace this development in Victorian Britain, in Europe and in the United States. Japan follows the same path but at a distance. Many of the Japanese former peasants are still at work. The changes brought about by the third and fourth generation have only just begun.

So far, Japan followed a known pattern. But it is an Oriental country and different in many ways from Germany or even from Russia. One important difference lies in the strength of the family or clan. The Japanese community is not a collection of individuals but of family groups. The individual matters less as such, being merely a passing phase in a continuing stream of life which includes both ancestors and descendants. The traditional Japanese emphasis on ritual suicide is to be understood in the context of a life pattern in which the individual counts for less than in Europe. The family matters more and that is why few Japanese women remain in the factory after marriage. As for the men, they have tended to transfer to the firm the sense of membership which they formerly derived from the extended family or village. If they thought of themselves as individuals, as helpless units in a hostile world, they would feel unhappily insecure. They prefer to be members of a family group, this preference having at least three important consequences. First of all, the employee has tended to stay in the same firm for his working life, no more thinking of deserting his firm than he would consider changing his name. Second, the status system within the firm (as within the family) lays a tremendous stress on seniority and on regular promotion or increment based on length of service. Third, the trade union has always been associated with the firm, not with the trade. It is, as it were, an extension or reflection of the firm, providing the basis for an internal negotiation but not inconsistent with a basic loyalty. Shintoism, the state religion of Japan, is distinct from other creeds in its emphasis on ancestor-worship. This reflects the idea of family solidarity and of the respect due to age. These attitudes must weaken in a highly mechanised and developing society but they have much to give Japan its enviable history of good industrial relations.

Japan has also a feudal background, the samurai wearing their distinctive swords until 1876 and retaining some prestige for long afterwards. Whether in Japan or Europe, feudalism never created the master-slave situation which journalists of to-day are apt to assume. Feudalism creates a web of mutual obligation on either side, the system maintained by a strong sense of loyalty. The legend of the forty ronin is not a story of one man's popularity but of forty men fulfilling a feudal duty. So recently was the system abolished that many elderly Japanese must have heard their fathers speak of it from personal experience. This tradition has also been absorbed into industrial practice, perhaps through the medium of the family firm.

Here again the tendency has been to stress the idea of loyalty; that of the men to the master being paralleled by that of the master to his men. There is a memory of feudalism in the fringe benefits which the Japanese employee will often receive; the big bonus paid twice a year, the living accommodation provided by the company, the free transport and the health services, the subsidised meals and sports facilities, the recreation centre in the mountains. This paternalistic treatment of employees goes with their permanence of employment. They are loyal but not unrewarded for their loyalty. In American terms they have tenure and the certainty, during good behaviour, of a measured advancement. In return for solid benefits they devote themselves to the firm's interests. This has been a key factor in Japanese prosperity.

A last influence in Japanese industry has been that of Buddhism, which can take many different forms. There is, however, a general Buddhist tendency to encourage meditation and simplicity. As compared with other peoples, the Japanese have had a rather austere style of living, their homes rather bare and small, their search being for tranquility rather than ostentation. There is little in Buddhist tradition to encourage anyone in the pursuit of wealth for its own sake. The Buddhist is rather inclined to accept his position in the world, being content with his salary and having no desire to set up a new business of his own. Generalisations about Buddhism are rash but it would seem to have an effect in curbing the more extreme forms of ambition. Many higher executives in Japan seem to be content with massive fringe benefits—apartments and cars, holidays and country-club membership—without seeking millionaire status. Some Japanese traditions, like the Tea Ceremony, or Flower arrangement, are complex as a performance but economical in cost. Japanese gardens are replete with symbolic meaning but involve only the inexpensive elements of stone, green vegetation and water, and these deployed in only a limited space. Traditional Japan has been a land of deliberate simplicity, one in which it has been easy to accept a middling way of life. Ideas are changing but Buddhism has so far been far from the Protestant Ethic.

In each of the features of Japanese life so far briefly described the big companies have, clearly, a wasting asset. Each generation moves further from the agricultural background, the family pattern, the feudal tradition and the religious belief. Industrial relations are already less tranquil and disorders are no longer unknown. And as these assets vanish Japan's original weaknesses must become more obvious. Japan is hopelessly overcrowded with little room even for industrial expansion. It lacks raw materials and depends for them on countries which may before long have none to export. It is without iron or oil and is overshadowed by China's weight of numbers. It is difficult to believe that Japan can for long sustain its position as a great Far Eastern Power. As against that, its initial momentum is far from spent. Its immediate future may well be prosperous and it is totally wrong to suppose that the Japanese are without powers of invention. If there was a period when they seemed to be copyists, that period is over and they are already surpassing those they used to emulate. For some years to come, perhaps for another generation, we shall find the Japanese formidable competitors. Whether we like it or not, we shall find ourselves buying their ships and cars, their cameras and lenses. They have yet to teach us something about the manufacture of steel and as much again about the standardisation of parts, which was in fact a Japanese idea. Americans who sought at one time to teach the Japanese about democracy ended by learning from them something about architecture. For years to come we shall look upon them with respect.

But what have we to learn from them now in terms of management? We cannot easily recreate the advantages

they have had. We cannot find recruits from the country-
side. We cannot revive feudalism or the family group. We
cannot convert each other to Buddhism. So what have we
to learn from them? To answer that the reader of this
foreword must go on to read the book, not forgetting the
summary at the end. But there are one or two points
which deserve mention at the beginning. First of all, the
Japanese begin with a good general education. They waste
little time on vocational training in the schools, believing
(and rightly) that a general education is what matters. The
result is that they are, as a nation, superbly literate. Books
of every kind are translated into Japanese and sold in
numbers which prove the existence of a highly intelligent
public. We might do well to burn our textbooks of educational theory and discover what the Japanese method is.
Whatever their practice, it is clearly better than ours. In
the second place, their custom has been to offer security of
employment, with increments for seniority and a regular
bonus for achievement. Theirs has been a great record of
industrial peace. Is security the key to that? It is certainly
one of them, as a recent book* has sufficiently proved. It
is a plan to which we should give serious thought. In the
third place, they retire most of their employees at the age
of 55–57 usually offering them further employment but at
a lower rate of pay. Exceptional in this respect are the
directors, who are mostly older than 55, contrasting with
the managers who can be a great deal younger. Here again
is a system which would repay careful study. In the fourth
and last place, the Japanese have in some firms a system of
annual self-evaluation. This would seem to be an extremely
valuable idea, worthy of prompt imitation. There is much
more to it than that, however, and the reader should now
read the book itself. He will end by realising that it is a
very good book indeed.

C. NORTHCOTE PARKINSON

*Industrial Disruption, Leviathan House, 1973.

Japanese Management

There are many who believe that modern industry is being governed by the law of increasing efficiency, and that it is therefore possible to set up generally accepted rules for this purpose. A study of non-European conditions, however, shows that while an economic system which responds to real market conditions, and at the same time is a profitable one, is beginning to emerge in all countries where freedom prevails, the ways of achieving this vary considerable.

For example, a comparison of conditions in Japan with those of Western Europe, shows that efficient management in Japan is tied to a different cultural system of values. Such a comparison contributes to a bettter understanding of Japanese achievements, strengths and weaknesses. At the same time it makes clearer the extent to which, in most Western countries, one is working on accepted but by no means obvious suppositions.

The success of any economic system in the eyes of others depends on these suppositions being clearly recognised and on their relative values being agreed.

The description of Japanese management in this book is based on personal investigations of the author into large-scale Japanese industry during the years 1965, 1966 and 1970, and on an extensive study of the literature on the subject.

The author's visits to Japan in 1965 and 1966 were mainly concerned with research into the working attitudes and living conditions of the industrial population. In September 1970 a visit was arranged for the specific purpose of carrying out research into the management structure of eight large Japanese firms. This type of research in Japan presented many problems, not the least being the language barrier, to a European with limited financial means. But it seemed especially necessary not to leave this sort of research to Japanese or even American experts, who might not be well acquainted with European conditions.

The chief areas of concern for the author during his investigations were the reliability of the data obtained and their relevance to an understanding of Japanese management, as seen through European eyes. The detailed studies which follow focus attention on typical similarities and differences in Japanese management methods.

This investigation is divided into three parts. First, the basic framework of Japanese management is described from economic, social and historic viewpoints. This introduction is essential to an understanding of peculiarities which are, in part, traditional.

In the second part the basic principles of management in large-scale Japanese industry are given, as derived from empirical studies. Typical characteristics which were found frequently recurring are given particular prominence.

The third part of the book describes the individual investigations of the author. These will enable readers to make their own personal judgments about Japanese industry, on the basis of facts about specific traces and their managerial peculiarities.

Finally, attention is drawn to the changes which are emerging and to those being anticipated, in management structure and practices in large-scale Japanese industry.

This publication would not have been possible without the help of the Japanese interpreters. To all of these the author would like to express his sincere thanks. Particular mention should be made of the assistance given by Dr. Reh and Mr. Bothe of the Efficiency Promotion Board of German Trade and Industry and also of Messrs. Kohei

Goshi, Yasushi Viva, Shotaro Nakumura and Akira Kana-
mori of the Japan Productivity Centre. They have all
assisted my investigations with great understanding. To
Professor Madame Nichiko Koyasu of the Waseda University of Tokyo, who was responsible for the major work
of translation, the author is especially grateful.

FRIEDRICH FÜRSTENBERG

Editor's Note on English Translation
Thanks are due to Mr. Denis Cooper and to Tek Trans-
lators for their meticulous work in translating from German
into English and to Mr. George Bell for his work in reducing
the amount of detail in the original text.

GEORGE COPEMAN

CHAPTER 1

The Background in Brief

Japan and Germany are industrial nations of the 'second generation'. They were forced to carry through their economic development while competing against powerful and experienced industrial nations and in a relatively short time, without any appreciable help from other countries. In each case the traditional forces of economic and social life led to new goals and new methods. The direction, range and success of the efforts involved were mainly due to the way that the ideas of the various social groups concerned were brought together.

The industrialisation of Japan was brought about at the time of the Meiji Restoration between 1868 and 1880 by a small executive group composed of the revolutionary younger samurai. Most of its members came from the aristocracy of south-west Japan, who had already had dealings with foreigners. To bring about this industrial re-construction, State-owned model factories, previously established for military purposes, were used.

Three groups of undertakings were involved: those of the Ministry of Industry; ironworks, wharves, chemical works and mines; those of the Ministry of Commerce and Agriculture; weaving and spinning mills and agricultural equipment; and those of the Department for Regional Development, which controlled 24 establishments necessary for bringing prosperity to the Hokkiado islands in Northern Japan. At the same time, considerable attention was given to the improvement of roads and to industrial training schemes.

To this end a great deal of use was made of Western

'know-how' and techniques. In 1876 the Ministry of Supply alone recruited 270 foreign experts. Costs were exceptionally high. One French engineer, for example, recruited by the Sumitomo Mining Co., earned six times as much as the managing director. Such situations led to the replacement of foreign experts by Japanese nationals as soon as possible. The Ministry of Education alone spent one-fifth of its budget on training Japanese workers. In 1873, 250 of the 373 Japanese who were studying abroad were receiving state aid.

A comparison with Germany during the same period shows that industrial development did not at first take place in Germany so quickly as in Japan. In spite of massive state assistance, the private element was the stronger in Germany. There was an active urban middle class of business people as well as a free farm-owning community.

In Japan, feudalism had by 1868 been extensively dissolved and contacts with the West broken so that traditional methods remained firmly anchored. This is shown in the Samurai influence on the formation of works management principles and in their continuation to this day, although in modified form.

The Samurai were strongly imbued with the idea of service and self-discipline. With the disintegration of the feudal Tokugawa-Shogunat, loyalty to the local lord was transferred to the nation and with it a spirit of enterprise, out of a sense of national duty. A form of revolutionary patriotism emerged, the aim of which was to spare Japan, having regard to the Chinese situation, from colonisation. This finds expression in the principles of the Samurai group: 'Fukoku Kychei' ('For a wealthy nation with a strong power of resistance').

The industrial revolution of Germany at about the same time, after the foundation of the Reich in 1871, was inspired by the Wilhelm patriotism. This created a climate of discipline not only among the workpeople, but also among the commercial and managerial classes.

In Japan the old trading class did not at first take part in the industrialisation. It maintained an ultra-conservative position and showed no inclination to look ahead or to take risks. This same state of affairs is apparent today among the developing nations. On the other hand the Samurai themselves proved incapable of adapting to private capitalistic ventures and they showed little talent for business.

Around 1880 the Japanese State, hard pressed for capital, sold to private industry, on extremely favourable terms, those undertakings which largely had been working at a loss. The enterpreneurs who took advantage of this opportunity were mostly families of traders, like the Mitsui and Mitsubishi. Others were wealthy farmers.

Until 1890, 55% of the leading manufacturing firms were owned by the trader classes and 40% by Samurai and the larger farmers. Furthermore, and this is important for the works management principles which gradually came into being, the Samurai held many key managerial posts in the developing family businesses (Zaibatsu).

Unlike the samurai, traders of the Tokugawa tradition were extremely 'house conscious', believing that profits should benefit the whole family, not just the individual. Profits were usually re-invested and this considerably restricted spending on luxury goods. The aim was the prosperity of the whole family and this stimulated a powerful economic drive. Thus the 'Iye principle' in Japan, to a considerable extent fulfilled the same function as was assumed in Western Europe by the principle of individual 'enlightened self-interest'. Without this background information the Zaibatsu, a typical form of family business, cannot be understood and its success cannot be explained.

Until the end of the Second World War we find in Japan, where family businesses prevailed, strong influences of the 'kazokushugiteki', or family approach to works management. Cases of inefficiency in family controlled management or lack of interest by succeeding generations, were handled in a variety of ways. For example, in the house of Mitsui the responsibilitites of actual management were given over to a 'banto', or general manager.

The Ko-Ko principle of the Tokugawa period set the pattern of behaviour for managerial staff in relation to the owner-family. This was a personal relationship based on a feeling of duty, arising from a feeling of gratitude. Personal devotion was the motivating force.

German businesses in the early days of industrialisation operated under much the same conditions and involved similar forms of personal indebtedness to the business-owning family. But, from the start there was a strong individualistic element. Even in family undertakings the dominating force of family tradition has never been so striking as in Japan.

Management principles in Germany reflected not so much family tradition or the ethics of the aristocracy, but rather the concept of the contract. With this was interwoven the model of a national bureaucracy, a sense of military discipline and an element of individual working ethics. However, as in Japan, industrial advance took place in the social and political climate of a late-feudal State. Here the focus of advance was not a liberal citizenship, such as obtained in England or France or to a much greater extent in the U.S.A., but the conservative forces.

Contrary to the relatively quick change in Germany, development in Japan proceeded more slowly and continuously up to the end of the Second World War. Many problems which confronted German management after 1918 only became realities in Japan after 1945. It is true that in Japan a 'revolution from the right' had taken place, combined with a pronounced tendency towards militarism. These events were, however, related to a continuous tradition of loyalty to the State which found its symbolic expression in the Emperor.

CHAPTER 2

Traditional Japanese Management Principles

Current management principles in Japan are largely the products of adaption of Japanese tradition to Western influences, the latter dominated by the American occupation. The realities of Japanese business life, particularly in big business, and the concepts which operate in it are made clear by these five basic principles. 1. Permanent employment. 2. The status system. 3. The seniority principle. 4. Compulsory early retirement, and 5. Collective decision-making. The numerous small undertakings evince marked paternalism, as is evident from the considerable number of unpaid members of the family.

1. *Permanent employment (Shushin-koya) of labour.* This is a special feature of Japanese large industrial firms. Workers undertake life-long employment for a company; for its part the company guarantees wages and employment for the full working life (shogai-fuye). Immobility of wage-earners (ko-in), contrary to a widely held view, was introduced only during the second phase of industrialisation, especially after the First World War, when there was a marked shortage of qualified workers.

In the earlier years of industrialisation, however, many factory workers were unskilled and they often included a very high proportion of females. In 1909, for example, 85% of the workers in the textile mills were women, and of these, 10% were children under the age of 14. This meant there was a high rate of turnover of the labour force. In the Fuji Gasu Boseki Kaishi spinning mill at Okyamaa, for example, 2,650 males and 13,150 women were employed in 1909. In the same year 2,104 men and 5,765 women left the company's employment. Only 259 workers had remained with the company for six years.

Since an adequately trained labour force is an absolute prerequisite to production on an internationally competitive scale, management has to resort to the patriarchal principle, still existing in Japanese government undertakings and in the old-established family-owned trading houses, which relied on a system of mutual obligations of employer and employee." They also adopted oyakata-kokata, a programme which firmly integrated foremen into the company's management, ensured their thorough training and through them the support of their workers. "

In these ways, between 1908 and 1918, the shushin-koyo principle developed. However its application was restricted by a three-tier system of employment in large-scale industry. In addition to the regular workers employed on a life-time basis (joyo-ko), a distinction is drawn between the auxiliary workers employed on a provisional or part-time basis (rinji-ko) and labourers (hiyatoi). Clearly the shushin-koyo principle comes from the needs of management and is not a primary policy of the work force itself. Management's total commitment is an offer to privileged groups of workers.

Labour turnover arising from movements of employees from one large firm to another is surprisingly low, though in the smaller firms the position is very similar to that in Europe. For companies employing more than 500 people the labour turnover rate in 1968 was 15·4% and for male workers alone, only 11%. Moreover the pattern of job changes was in keeping with the system of a three-tier workforce.

The principle of permanent employment includes a no-dismissal clause agreed to by management but it does not morally oblige a worker to remain with one enterprise. However, only by staying with one company can a worker obtain the privileges which go with length of service. Thus it is a question of a management principle based on practical advantages rather than on commitment.

It must be frankly admitted that guaranteed employment enables a company to retain qualified and skilled workers. Moreover, the workers show little resistance to rationalisation of their work, since they enjoy almost unlimited rights against dismissal.

On the other hand, the immobility of the permanent staff exerts tremendous pressure for promotion to the higher jobs and this has led to them being over-filled. It also causes the creation of numerous substitutes for advancement, so that the work relationship of the permanent staff is not so much contract-oriented as status-oriented.

While the status system guarantees a job even to the less competent workers, it can and does lead to considerable tension and dissatisfaction. However, a personal evaluation system to determine future social status is used as a 'lubricant', to promote efficiency within the framework of the permanent employment system. The principle of Shushin-koya also restrains ambition for a personal career, in favour of the idea of working for the good of the firm. Loyalty is focused on the undertaking itself.

Observers from other nations often maintain that Shushin-koya is contrary to the needs of a dynamic management which, in adapting itself to market conditions, should have a flexible labour force. However, in addition to the permanently employed staff in Japanese firms, there are workers engaged only on short-term contracts. Also many large Japanese businesses put out much of their work under sub-contract and have no responsibility for the people who actually do the work.

Finally, any rigidity which might result from guaranteed employment in the face of fluctuating market requirements is largely avoided by a system of flexible bonus payments which are related to output.

Another problem inherent in every guarantee of employment is the potentially high ratio of old people to the total work force. This is overcome, however, by the system of compulsory early retirement which is discussed later in the book. Also, pensions are relatively high, compared with basic wages. Japanese trade unions support the shushin-koya principle largely because it causes continuous over-manning and undoubtedly because it has brought greatly improved living conditions to Japan, but only, it should be remembered, for a privileged class of employees.

2. *The Mibun or Status principle.* Japanese management has traditionally embraced this principle. Until the Second World War employees in large Japanese firms were divided into two widely differing groups: the shoku-in, or salary earners and administrative personnel, and the ko-in, or wage-earners. The shoku-in largely identified themselves with the company and its achievements and were, in European eyes, beneficiaries of an extreme paternalism. The large masses of ko-in were by contrast subjected to impersonal and less humanitarian forms of industrial discipline. The Mibun principle, however, was gradually subjected to question by the disproportionate increase in white collar workers and by the raising of the general standard of education. These levelling-up tendencies were further reinforced by the Second World War.

The post-war period brought a further softening of the Mibun principle by the introduction of status qualifications based on education and years of service (Shikaku-seido). The continual raising of the education level, however, soon rendered this system questionable. More recently, qualifications based on job function have been increasingly introduced (shokuno-batau shikaku-seide).

Nonetheless, the old status system has often remained in operation. Thus foreigners get the impression of a two-way hierarchy in Japan whereby the status and the functional systems are separated, yet in a very complex way are dependent on one another. In Western Europe also there are many distinctions between social grades, particularly between white collar workers and industrial or blue collar workers. But these differences are being steadily eroded under a policy of treating all employees alike. This trend appears to be taking place in Japan as well.

3. *The Nenko-joretsu or Seniority principle.* While the principle of a life-time of permanent employment at one firm has been relaxed, it is nevertheless set as an example to be followed. Also it is closely connected with Nenko-joretsu, the Seniority principle. In Japan, length of service with one company is still the decisive factor in determining an employee's position in his firm, his rights and the treatment he can expect. It has a particular bearing on pay and promotion.

In Japanese industry wages and salaries are determined by education, age and the number of years an employee has worked. There are also numerous supplementary payments, but these are only partly related to individual performance. The wage incentive in large industrial undertakings is first and foremost the individual's reward for long-term performance.

The incentive for higher output works indirectly and is long-term. Against this background one can see the difficulties of introducing into large-scale Japanese undertakings a European wage and salary system based on immediate performance and evaluation of work.

Permanent employment, of course, restricts the employee's career to a single undertaking. There are few exceptions to this. Top management in large Japanese companies who have advanced by virtue of having worked in other enterprises are very rare.

Promotion according to length of service has an interesting consequence. The senior managers in Japanese industry are mainly those with long service. People with the same experience and the same educational background are able to develop a special group consciousness. This creates, however, some problems. Few Japanese managers are used to cooperating with younger colleagues of equal standing. One side effect is that it is extremely difficult for Western companies with young managements to engage qualified Japanese managers.

4. *Teinen or Compulsory Early Retirement principle.* The principle of compulsory retirement at a relatively early age, 55 to 57 years (Teinen-seido) is not new. It has long been the Japanese custom to retire no later than the age of 50, but modern industrial conditions have brought about a significant rise in the retirement age. When the principle of permanent employment was introduced large industrial companies adopted compulsory retirement rather than dismiss those whose efficiency or work contribution had been steadily decreasing as a result of advancing years. Thus the principle of early retirement has brought the average age of the Japanese working population down to a relatively low level. Exceptions to early retirement are sometimes made for senior administrative personnel who are allowed to continue working.

After compulsory retirement, employees are often re-employed on a temporary basis (shoku-taku) and mostly in subsidiary companies. This practice of dismissing employees at retirement age and immediately re-engaging them at reduced salaries and under different conditons clearly shows the important role which dismissal plays in creating opportunities for those whose careers are restricted by the policy of permanent employment. In 1967, 69% of all Japanese companies were operating a system of early retirement. For firms with 500 or more employees the percentage was 93·7.

On retirement at the age of 55 to 57 an employee gets a lump sum equal to one month's pay for every year of service. In spite of this the economic position of early retirees often becomes difficult during the waiting time of several years before they become eligible for State pensions. Even then, the majority of old age State pensioners are also the recipients of special social security benefits. Those in receipt of contributory pensions amount to only 29% of the total. In fact pension payments to those over 65 amount to only 12·9% of the income of the total population.

Apparently the system of compulsory early retirement functions because the large family businesses continue to accept people over the age of 55.

5. *The Ringi, or Collective decision-making principle.* Probably the most remarkable Japanese management principle is the collective decision-making (ringi) principle. Where do the responsibilities of an individual executive lie in relation to this principle?

Imagine a mature gentleman in a top-level office studying a report. He adds a few observations, gives it his personal approval and then passes it on. The system behind this action operates approximately as follows:

(1) Any plan or suggestion (ringisho), from whatever source, is prepared and worked out in detail at middle management level.

(2) Before the plan is submitted to higher management all relevant departments of middle management subject it to close examination and they may modify it, sometimes after general discussion.

(3) Acceptance of the plan does not depend on its receiving approval at a particular level in the company. The plan is likely to be given approval in a prescribed form and in sequence at various executive levels.

(4) In many companies the managing director is the person who finally agrees the plan which, on its way to him, may have been provided with a dozen or more

approvals, so that any individual responsibility is difficult to locate.

It may be thought that this method of decision-making amounts to complete abrogation of responsibility. But such an interpretation is fallacious. Decisions are planned and carried out by middle management who are allowed a great deal of discretion and hence of responsibility. Moreover, everyone concerned has a hand in shaping decisions. This aspect of the decision process is given special emphasis. Obstructionism is thus largely avoided.

One must therefore agree with W. H. Brown, the American observer, who states: 'It is precisely this group orientation of the managers, their team work and the existence of harmonious personal relations, which give to Japanese organisations their strength and efficiency. This type of organisation does not suppress the special capabilities of an individual. It allows him the broadest possible scope. The faults of a person, likewise, are obscured, since they are counter-balanced by the strengths of his colleagues. Finally a feeling of group satisfaction is engendered because each one contributes to the vital activity of the undertaking and shares in it.'

In large European companies, responsibility for decisions is firmly located in one person who can be called to account for them. At least this is the view of most people as to how the system works. In practice, however, things are often quite different. Usually several people participate in the decision-making process and specialist advisers are becoming increasingly important. The actual difference between the Japanese system and the European is probably only slight and it lies in the official emphasis on the role of the individual in Europe, in contrast to the role of the group in Japan. Both points of view have strong and weak points. The Japanese system doubtless functions very well in some cases. Moreover, though the Ringi system is the dominant one, other decision-making methods are also employed by the Japanese.

The basic principles of permanent employment which have been outlined, the system of status differentiation, promotion and remuneration in accordance with years of service, compulsory retirement and group-orientated decision-making are the most common differences between Japanese and European managements. They are closely associated with various traditions which derive from the attitudes and behaviour standards of the social classes controlling the process of industrialisation. They are also affected by a special characteristic of the Japanese labour market, which until recently had an excessive supply of labour, so that managements were able to negotiate from a position of strength.

In contrast, the stronger individualistic view of working capacity and the more formal nature of management structure appear to be the main features of business in Europe. Industrial relationships in Europe are also more formal than in Japan. They are not so much based on the co-operation of groups with shared values but on the purposeful co-operation and conflict of groups seeking their own ends. In Europe, society on entering the age of industrialisation was already more strongly individualistic and the conception of the business firm as the extended family had already diminished.

CHAPTER 3

Reforms After 1945

Today the old Japanese management traditions continue in the major firms, in large measure. This indicates that reforms introduced after the Second World War have only modified conditions, not altered them crucially. The reforms have in fact especially favoured large-scale industry whose influence on the economic and social structure of Japan has been greatest.

The measures taken by the American occupation powers in the first few years after the war sought to bring about a more efficient and more democratic way of Japanese society and economic life. They were directed towards marketing methods, improvement of business competition by anti-monopoly legislation and the abolition, in the first instance, of excessive concentration of economic power —aimed especially against those parts of large-scale industry which were organised as Zaibatsu. The disentanglement of these family businesses proved, however, to be relatively ineffective, and for two reasons.

First, the occupying forces were interested in the speedy rehabilitation of an efficient large-scale Japanese industry for political reasons. At the latest, by the beginning of the Korean war, industry was able to go its own way without any significant difficulties. Second, the integration of Japan into the world economy was possible only by the employment of modern production methods which pre-supposed a considerable concentration of capital. Thus the Zaibatsu undertakings were reorganised and large-scale Japanese industry generally was promoted by extensive

Government credits and generous import facilities for highly efficient plant and machinery.

The Japanese home market for industrial equipment favoured the introduction of new methods to obtain quick results, but at the same time, made it possible for efficient groups of companies to plan on a long-term basis to overcome strategic marketing difficulties.

The beginnings of democratic industrial working relations, through progressive legislation and freer action for the trade unions, proved to be more lasting. Especially in State undertakings and in large-scale industry, it was possible to set up stable trade union organisations. The trade union movement did contribute towards the partial modernisation of management in the large undertakings, but without appreciably shaking its fundamental conceptions; outside big industrial concerns it was mainly ineffectual.

In Japanese agriculture the reforms all led to a modernisation of agrarian production by the abolition of the old system of land tenure. Subsidies were given to encourage production, which led to the agricultural sector being able in the long term to release more and more workers to other sectors of the economy.

In the first post-war period the move to democratic methods of government doubtless turned out to be an appreciable impetus to modernisation and it had lasting effects on both large-scale industry and agriculture. But the pressure to modernise industry, as in Western Germany, soon built up an impetus of its own. Productive achievement became of paramount importance. Reconstruction developed its own dynamic and the democratic reforms became of secondary importance.

At the conclusion of the reconstruction phase of Japanese large-scale industry, a strong trend towards economic growth set in which led to the gross national product doubling between 1956 and 1961. In this period the number of workers rose annually by 10% and the agricultural population decreased by about two million. Then between 1960 and 1969, the gross national product increased by an annual rate of 11·1% but the employed population by only 1·4% a year. Consequently more people were looking for jobs, especially school leavers. These spectacular developments made themselves felt in world markets through the presence of Japanese products and there was much discussion abroad about the causes of this extraordinary economic boom.

Undoubtedly the principal cause was the great increase in Japanese large-scale industry. Coupled with this, of course, was the typical attitude towards work. The key position of large-scale industry in the expansion process proved to be all the more effective since, not only was the application of capital to technical innovations demanded by the government being justified, but in the struggle for a larger share of world markets, the Japanese national conscience saw its own efforts being realised and was thereby stimulated to even greater efforts.

The following factors are stressed as being particularly conducive to expansion:

(1) An appropriate government financial and monetary policy to make an extraordinarily large amount of capital available from which, primarily, the large firms could profit.

(2) The introduction of technical innovations in those industries with particularly high potential rates of growth such as machinery manufacturing, shipbuilding, electrical equipment and petrochemicals.

(3) Employment of a 'dual' economic structure to enable large-scale industry to obtain replacement and spare parts at extraordinarily low prices, the basis for this being the high degree of dependence of small and medium-sized firms on large-scale industry. In addition

to their relatively low capitalisation as compared to large-scale industry, manufacturers of predominantly labour-intensive products have the advantage of a relatively low level of wages since they employ a high proportion of women, older workers and unskilled workers from rural areas. The extraordinary success of Japanese large-scale industry has been largely due to the low-cost work of small and medium-sized industrial firms and their workers.

(4) Economic growth has been due in large measure to the continual freeing of agricultural workers, thus enabling large companies to engage them on a selective basis. In 1955, 40·5% of all workers were engaged in agriculture. Only 14 years later this proportion had fallen to 18·8%.

(5) Finally, the systematic development of the home market by State subsidies has ensured a relatively high level of demand and thus smoothed out the peaks of prosperity. (In 1969 exports were valued at only 9·4% of the gross national product.)

At present Japan is faced with a considerable backlog of work in building new towns and cities and this, together with the demand for a higher standard of living, generates further growth which helps to even out the effects of world economic fluctuations.

Among the significant innovations which have influenced the structure of Japanese large-scale companies in the post-war period is the Board system, adopted from the American model. It determines the management structure of limited companies, of which about 4,100 each have a capital of more than 100 million yen.

Under Japanese company law, shareholders are responsible in general meeting for the setting up and changing, where necessary, of the company's capital structure. The Board of Directors, who must be at least three, are selected

by the shareholders for a term of two years and are responsible for the basic planning of the firm's progress. In
addition the auditors have statutory responsibilities and a
fourth authority, the Management, are composed of representatives of the Board, appointed for two years and
responsible for the actual management. The chairman of
the Board is frequently also chairman of the Management
Committee. As a general rule the Directors and members
of the Management are identical, except that any directors
who have functional or departmental responsibilities are
subordinate to the managing director.

In Japan there is no independence for the Management
in the running and controlling of the business. In Continental Europe generally, however, Managements and
Boards of Directors are separate entities. In both cases the
influence of general meetings of shareholders is very small.

In Japanese limited companies the auditors have
largely a formal significance. They are usually appointed
in an honorary capacity and are very elderly. The actual
supervision of business policies and practices is carried out
by the banks who supply the credit or by their representatives. This supervision is not, however, concerned with
the detailed working methods of top management but with
the success of its activities in terms of profit. Thus the
Board system used in Japan, which in practice is rather
similar to that used in Britain, has given large-scale
Japanese firms a significant amount of freedom which is
not available to the same extent in Continental Europe
where the banks are usually represented on the supervisory
board—in those countries where there is one.

The relatively strong position of Japanese large-scale
industry in the country's economic life is also indicated by
the system of industrial relations. In 1945 legislation was
passed which guaranteed to Japanese workers the right to
join together in unions and the right to strike. Such
freedom of action had never before existed. The Working

Standards Act, passed in 1947, was of similar fundamental importance. It laid down minimum requirements relating to dismissal, safety and health, holidays, intervals for meals and among other things, rest periods at work.

In January 1946 the Trades Union Association, Sodomei, founded in 1920, was re-established. The following August, the National Congress of Industrial Trades Unions (Sambetsu) was formed and in March 1947 the National Trades Union Council (Zenrenkyo). These latter two were under strong communist influence, which led to their dissolution in 1955. The Sohyo organisation, an anti-communist successor, was formed in the same year but it subsequently proved to be troubled with conflicts between left-wing socialists and communists on the one hand and moderate socialists on the other. The moderates broke away and this led to the formation of the Japanese Trades Union Council (Zenro) which, in November 1964, combined with Sodomei to become the Domei.

At present Sohyo, with 37·8% of all trade union members and Domei, with 17·4% are the two largest unions. Domei is known for its ideological neutrality and its efforts to improve working conditions. Sohyo continues to pursue general social and political aims. These, however, vary from time to time, depending on the degree of influence of radical groups within the union.

It was the blatant radicalism of internal groups which led to the exhaustion of the Japanese trade union movement in struggles to determine its own policies. The unions were unable to develop an organisation consistent with the needs of highly organised modern economic life and unable to bring about fundamental reforms in working conditions, especially wages.

The significance of the trade unions and their influence on working conditions in large-scale companies only becomes clear if one appreciates their basic method of organisation. The overwhelming majority of unions are

'house' or company unions (Kigyobetsu Kumisi), membership of which in general is restricted to permanent
employees. In 1969 there were 58,818 unions with a total
membership of 11,248,601, or 35·2% of the Japanese
working population. As in Europe, union representation
varies directly with the size of the company, being greatest
in large firms and least in the smallest. It is significant that
unions in private industry tend towards membership of the
moderate Domei association which has grown continually
since 1967. Sohyo, which is mainly supported by public
service employees, appears to be stagnating.

Japanese company unions have rarely had enough
membership to equip themselves financially for pursuing
any far-reaching policies. For this reason they mostly lack
professional union leaders and experts. In general the
union leaders must remain employees of their particular
firm, to whom they continue to feel under obligation. After
giving up active union duties they can move into salaried
staff status or junior management, provided their 'conduct'
was satisfactory during their term of office.

If one considers the type of agreements negotiated
between employers and unions then their limited scope
becomes obvious. Japanese collective agreements (dantai
kyokaku) contain only the general confirmation of the
legality of the union, within the meaning of the trade union
legislation, and a declaration of intent to create friendly
relations between unions and management. During wage
negotiations, which are usually annual, the wages *system* is
not discussed; negotiation is restricted to the percentage
increase in the total wages bill to be paid during the coming
year, hours of work and rest periods during the working
day. Details of the working conditions are generally settled
by works rules (shugo kisoku) laid down by the employer
only, though individual works rules and orders may
become the subject of collective agreements.

By and large, Japanese company unions take action

similar to that of the parties to industry-wide wages agreements in Europe, but really effective action, as allowed by law, is rare. One special problem, resulting from the splitting of the Japanese trade union movement into separate and competing organisations, is the need for co-ordination of union activities with the aim of getting as many uniform wage settlements agreed for large sections of the economy as possible. Two policies which originated with the trade union Sohyo point the way. In 1952 a specific Japanese form of struggle for wages, 'gurumi', was introduced. Here the tactics of the Chinese communists were adopted. The aim was to strengthen the position of the unions by broadening public support. This was to be achieved by organising workers' families and engaging in other local communal activities. These attempts misfired.

A second attempt by Sohyo was more successful in motivating the Japanese unions at least once a year to launch a prepared and co-ordinated action. This was the so-called 'Spring Wage Offensive' (shungki chin-age kyodo bosi-shunto). The intention to strike and the wage demands of the participating unions are made known to the general public and the strikes then actually take place. Usually workers down tools only for short periods in protest actions intended to indicate their negotiating strength. Longer strikes are made more difficult by lack of union funds as well as the likelihood of some workers and all salaried staff quitting their company union and forming a new union to enable them to continue working. Moreover, there is in Japan an arbitration law to deal with such emergencies. The actual outcome of the Spring Wage Offensive is generally a compromise between the employers' proposals to base annual, individual rises on the existing wages and salaries and union demands for an all-round percentage increase.

Clearly the Japanese trade unions are limited in their effectiveness and they contribute little towards narrowing

the difference in wages which results from the dual economic structure between large-scale industry on the one
hand and medium and small firms on the other. Moreover,
the unions are essentially ineffective against a drop in real
wages and can do little to change the wages system or
working conditions. This means that the large-scale
companies have an almost free hand to make working
conditions fit the ideas of management. Not surprisingly
most of the unions come to terms with these conditions.
An additional factor is the traditional Japanese refusal
to make society an open battle ground, which is tem-
pered only by the desire to secure their interests by contract.

In some large-scale firms there have been moves towards
more positive consultations with the unions. One way is by
the setting up of joint works councils. In 1968 the Japan
Productivity Centre found that of 433 such councils, 6·7%
were union-prompted, 22% had been instigated by
management and the rest by mutual agreement. It appears
that the unions favoured the British model of joint consultation rather than the German model of works councils
with statutory rights, since under the old British system no
binding agreements are made. The problems of this type
of consultation are that they are seen by the workers as a
way towards greater union influence, yet managements
seek to use them to prevent this.

Social status is also playing a more important part in
the lives of Japanese workers, a growing number of whom
feel they belong to the middle class of society. The
Industrial Relations Centre of the Rikkyo University in
Tokyo has established that about 70% of the workers in
large-scale companies in private industry and about 65%
of those in public service identify themselves with the
middle classes. This may be due largely to the conviction
that the aims of the Socialist party are behind the times.
Whilst in 1962, 72·2% of the steel union (tekkoe roren)

members were Socialist party supporters, this figure had fallen to 23·4% by 1969.

Clearly the tendency of the workers to shape their own private lives has increased and greater importance is now attached to personal hobbies, recreation and family life. Nonetheless, among workers in large-scale industry who feel they belong to the middle class, there is no general lack of interest in union affairs. At the same time, satisfaction with union activities has lessened. This dissatisfaction may be ascribed to the critical, sceptical and at times cynical attitude which goes with improved education, the increase in mass culture and to some extent to growing individualism. These changes are being reflected in the new attitude of workers whose demands are going beyond the traditional emphasis on wages and hours. The unions are being pressed to bring about satisfactory conclusions to such problems as accommodation, social security, welfare, voluntary social contributions, better working conditions, more free time, holidays, overtime and recreation.

Finally, the workers in increasing numbers expect the unions to concern themselves actively with the engagement of labour, promotion, skill and vocational training. Overall, therefore, it can be seen that in the promotion of the trade union movement in Japan after the second world war, social revolutionary forces were less in evidence than the strong desire to co-operate with managements, certainly in the large companies.

Reorganisation of Japanese management since 1945 was under the powerful influence of the United States. At the end of 1947 the Supreme Command of the Allied Forces (SCAF) began organising and providing training for Japanese economic experts. For middle management, Management-Training-Programme (MTP) was organised and for lower management the well known programme, Training Within Industry (TWI) was provided. American teaching methods—case studies and group discussions—

were adopted by the large companies who gradually set
up their own training centres. The best known, the Hitachi
Company training centre, opened in June 1962, modelled
on that of General Electric in Crotonville, U.S.A. The
Toyota and Tishiba schemes are also considered exem-
plary.

Work Factor Methods were adopted quickly by Japanese industry while the 'productivity movement' based on
the European pattern was of special and lasting importance for contact with American management methods.

At the instigation of the United States, the Japan
Productivity Council was formed in June 1954. Three
months later the Japanese Cabinet put this on a permanent
basis by forming the Japanese Productivity Centre and
financing it from the national budget. By the following year
trade unionists were represented in the centre's administration.

For the first time in 1955 a team of top managers went
to the United States. Since then, assisted by the Centre,
nearly 10,000 foreign study journeys have been made by
management and union representatives. In reverse, about
200 American specialists have been to Japan in an advisory
or teaching capacity, to apply American management
methods.

The Japanese Productivity Centre has eight regional
centres, each of which holds regular courses on management training. Subjects offered are Marketing, Production
Management, Accountancy, Personnel Management,
Decision-making, Management Information Systems and
Manpower Development. The Centre also publishes
translations of American management books and it
attaches much importance to the training of industrial
advisers for individual firms.

The extent to which American management methods
are seen as a special and peculiar feature running counter
to traditional Japanese methods is clear from an address

given by Yoshima Ishikawa, director of the Japanese Management Association in Tokyo in 1969. He made the point that there were two contrary but co-existing management systems, 'Japanese' and 'American', and he supported the view that each system must remain as a separate entity, if it is to be applied successfully. But it was possible to apply both systems with advantage in the same company. This presupposes two types of activities in each undertaking, routine jobs and jobs which demand expertise. Accordingly, the work force tends to consist of two groups—the higher qualified group employed on a permanent basis and most suited to Japanese management methods and the older workers nearing retirement who are especially suited to American management methods.

Ishikawa concluded with the observation: 'By applying both types of management in this way an undertaking may effectively gain the advantages of both systems'. Thus it seems that the adoption of American management methods has not brought about any significant change in the independent stand taken by Japanese management. Where, for reasons of expediency, foreign methods have been adopted, there is a tendency to neutralise their 'reforming effect' by setting up a dual system.

Because of this basic attitude, attempts at reform since 1945 have certainly modified the fundamentals of Japanese management but have not brought about any decisive change in the system. Japanese managements in large companies have been able to absorb the many and various external influences into the dynamic Japanese economy and its own type of company system. They have done this in such a way that their own fundamental convictions, based on traditional conceptions, have continued to hold sway.

CHAPTER 4

Society and Service

It is remarkable the extent to which the main objectives of large Japanese firms reflect a harmonious basic concept of modern economic society. In the same way market relations are interpreted as mutual obligations, leading to a sharing of interests, and the social obligations of a company are stressed. Success in business, seen from this angle, is the result of the co-operation of all concerned and is a consequence of a balanced relationship between the undertaking and its environment. The ideologies of the working community include service to the general public and identify employees with the company. Sanyo, a medium-sized Japanese chemical firm, has the motto: 'Let us create a better society through the company'. To this end it aims to (1) Achieve rapid growth. (2) Have cordial relations throughout the firm. (3) Gain improved working efficiency. (4) Obtain more business by introducing original and high quality goods to the market. (5) Give value for money by offering excellent products at reasonable prices.

The company believes that the achievement of these aims must result in a substantial profit, to the benefit of the firm, its shareholders, management and employees. It believes service is the foundation of its existence.

Western observers may conclude that, in the same way as the individual worker does not give priority to the pursuit of individual aims, so the company is not to be seen as an individual unit in the economic process. The bond of the worker to the company is matched by the latter's obligation to operate within a framework of 'larger families of firms', which represent Japanese national success.

This picture of a monolithic national production organisation extensively integrated by harmonising contrasting views is, however, exaggerated. Even when competition is played down by integration ideologies, and this happens frequently because of its inhibiting effects on trade union solidarity, it is what happens in practice which really matters. Individual units having independent aims are not so much in competition with one another, as are groups of firms competitive within a wider market. 'Competition' in the Japanese sense should be more correctly described as 'sectionalism'. The point of competition is first and foremost to obtain an increased share of the market and so stimulate growth of the firm, but the small firm is likely to be working for a big group which is itself battling for a bigger market from which all may benefit.

It is interesting to look at the way in which the Japanese 'solve' the strained relationship between flexibility in competition and social stability of the company. Social integration and stability are considered pre-requisite to economic success and have a decided priority, yet in 1969 a poll of 713 firms showed that the solution of economic problems was clearly given more priority than improvement in morale of the workforce. Japanese management has dual objectives: firstly, management's search for opportunities of growth; and secondly, the harmonisation of social relations within a company, as well as between it and the environment. Contrary to the predictions of Western experts, the development of industrial capitalism in Japan has not led to the dual objectives disintegrating under the pressure of competition.

CHAPTER 5

Principles of Organisation

The organisation charts of Japanese firms give relatively clear information about their structure. Departments are fairly well defined, but not the status, authority and responsibilities of their members. During the early postwar period supervision was highly centralised but it has been gradually changed by two developments in large-scale companies. Stronger staff organisations were formed, product groups with their own budgets were promoted in conjunction with increased efforts at cost control. Usually only large-scale undertakings have separate and relatively independent divisions for each group of products.

As with European companies, the organisation of operating units depends on the size of the company and on the types of products. The 1969 poll showed that only 16·7% of the companies questioned considered changes toward an operating unit system of organisation to be necessary.

The peculiarities of functional organisation in major Japanese firms stem from the fact that the work and status of an executive are almost inseparable. Without a knowledge of the particular status of the employee, organisation often seems hypothetical. Moreover, because of the many Japanese decision-making processes (ringi systems), it is difficult to recognise performance differences and decision delegation in any plan modelled on a Western pattern. These limitations are evident from the following table:

Upper management

Chairman of the Board of Directors	Kaicho
President	Schacho
Vice-president	Fauk-scacho
General manager	Senmu
Manager	Jomu
Director (boardroom title)	Torishimariyaku
Accountant	Jonin-Kansayaku
Auditor	Kansayaku

Middle Management

Chief departmental manager	Bucho
Deputy chief departmental manager	Fuko-Bucho
Departmental head	Kacho

Lower Management

Group manager	Kararicho
Foreman	Shokucho (Sunin)
Supervisor	Kumicho (Fuku-shunin)

Top management generally embodies the posts from director upwards. It forms the Board of Directors which, however, seldom meets in its entirety and which does not generally make major decisions. The most important decisions are made at the meetings of the Chairman, the President and the vice-President. While fundamental decisions are made by the inner circle of top management, lower levels of managerial meetings decide on the application and execution of basic programmes. Some major Japanese companies also appoint special groups to deal with specific tasks.

In spite of the foregoing, top executives in no way allow themselves to be restricted by formal rules when taking decisions and in this respect they follow the example of their Western counterparts. To assist them they have expert staffs to advise in the making of their decisions, the preparation of long-term plan techniques and the development of management information systems (MIS).

The growth of staff in the major companies has brought problems, particularly in respect of their productive use. To encourage staffs to be more productive, the Japan Management Association in 1967 put forward a Management of Indirect Costs Plan (MIC). Its main points were:— greater incentives and work application planning to achieve comparable performance standards, and greater flexibility of office staff. Lack of flexibility often arose because staff posts generally were allotted to departments without any real examination of need and in many cases a career was confined to the one department.

While the department chief had clearly defined promotion prospects before him, promotion for specialists was much less likely. An attempt was made to remedy this situation by setting up a functional hierarchy for experts. In practice, the positions to which the specialists were promoted frequently lacked authority. However, advancing rationalisation, particularly the application of electronic data processing, must result in a revaluation of staff posts and consequently a fundamental change in functional staff jobs.

In lower management, the position of foreman has also posed many problems in Japanese heavy industry. Until about 1958, the foreman worked on strict instructions from the manager and was responsible for training. Often he was the immediate leader of a working group. This was recognised during the revival of the trade union movement after the Second World War. It became necessary to improve the standard of lower management before integration with total management could take place.

The introduction of the American foreman system from about 1958 served this purpose, the major steel firms acting as pacemakers. The new type of foreman (Sogyocho) is expressly and formally recognised as a member of lower management.

Problems also arose for departmental organisation which had difficulty in communicating with other departments because of the firm boundaries dividing them. Only one third of the managers interviewed on the subject maintained that their top executive organisation operated with almost no problems.

The difficulties obviously arose from differences in social status, dependence on the decisions of higher levels and lack of authority during detailed procedure meetings when several levels of the executive and staff hierarchies were involved. The methods used to try and overcome these problems reflect modern management doctrines the world over.

The functional organisation of major Japanese companies cannot be understood without knowing the status problems. In Japanese heavy industry there are traditional barriers between the white collar employees in offices or engaged in technical work, and on the other hand, the production workers. Changes in education and in business methods, however, have altered this system so radically that in some companies the status of employees in both sections is the same. The influence of the seniority system has been repressed but not finally broken.

CHAPTER 6

Information and Decision-Making

For general internal information, the methods and aids used in major Japanese companies are similar to those used in Europe. Most important is personal contact between executives and workers either informally or through conferences. Emphasis is, of course, placed on group development, section leaders being called upon to improve communications within their section. Wherever a large proportion of the workers live in company-owned accommodation, relationships between workers are relatively close, and so, to some extent, are relations between workers and immediate superiors. Thus discussions on business problems can be continued after working hours. At Toyota, for instance, conferences at workshop level frequently take place outside working hours, as do group meetings chaired by executives.

A form of communication frequently used in Japanese companies is the so-called 'Voluntary Reporting System', a self-criticism of the worker, using a questionnaire. This provides information about the work, interests and problems of each particular person, his ambitions, proposals or ideas and his dislikes, if any, relating to his present employment. The information thus collected makes an important contribution to personnel planning.

In addition, top management try to reach specific groups within middle management and the work force by memoranda, information sheets and works newspapers. The latter appeal greatly to many workers and foster a team spirit which helps to promote a fighting, competitive attitude. Also remarkable are the numerous publications by Japanese companies for their customers and a wider public. These serve as public relations media and are international in form and content.

Compared to European practice, personnel departments play a very important part in the total information system which, according to Japanese business philosophy, has a special role in the business organisation. Clearly the systematic collection and dissemination of information by Japanese companies is part of their radical modernisation programme and the traditional file and card index systems for reports and documentation are being brought up to date by the use of computer systems.

Obviously middle management plays a key role in evaluating information, but since only about one-in-three of the managers consulted in this study referred to the value of the information system for management decision-making and only about one-in-four considered that managers were given accurate information, it seems that the information flow has shortcomings.

It should be remembered, however, that a glut of information and vested departmental interests are not conducive to an optimum consideration of information by over-worked managers, a problem which arises in all major organisations, and is in no way typically Japanese. Japanese companies are making an effort to develop modern management information systems, but this will require much time and perseverance.

A recent survey by the Ministry for Foreign Trade and Industry (MITI) on the use of operations research methods showed that they are used extensively in long-term planning and more especially in production planning, and that general statistical methods and simulation processes prevailed over linear programming and PERT (programme evaluation and review technique). Operations research methods are to a large extent but not always employed in conjunction with a computer system. In the past computer systems have been used primarily for wage calculations, order processing systems and other day-by-day operations and only secondarily for analysis, planning and forecasting work. This situation is likely in the future to be reversed.

There seems to be an irreconcilable contradiction between modern management information systems based on computers and traditional Japanese decision-making practice (the ringi system). The tiresome ringi approval procedure is becoming superfluous but in major Japanese companies it is still regarded as of considerable, and sometimes fundamental importance. The ringi system is gradually losing its decision-making functions and is being converted to an information medium and an approval procedure based on comments. Also the ringi system tends to be used only for medium and long-term projects or for routine administrative decisions and it is being used to explain points of view.

A natural result of the intense group consciousness of Japanese management is that at least all who are concerned in the development of modern computer information systems and all who are concerned with retaining the ringi system come within the consultative procedure for administrative decisions and for decisions on long-term projects. The problem is to combine the trend towards using modern computer systems for decision-making with the advantages of conventional group consultation activities. The logic of the ringi system lies in the fact that agreement is based on information exchange and discussion among all participants. It should therefore be capable of being incorporated in modern management information and decision-making systems.

CHAPTER 7

Planning and Research

Long-term planning is increasingly becoming recognised by large Japanese companies as a fundamental task of management. A good example of detailed planning is the Showa-Denko-Long-Range-Planning System (SLORPS) in which a financial plan, a sales plan and a cost-efficiency calculation for the production plant are combined. The projections thus calculated for long-term growth and the development of profitability and liquidity serve as a basis for decision-making which is, however, suitably adapted to changing circumstances.

Another company, Mitsubishi Chemical Industries Ltd., use a special team of experts to draw up their five-year development plan, collect the data and evaluate it. They face extremely difficult co-ordination problems created by the very existence of a central planning department. Apart from the difficulty of accurately predicting world influences on their markets, the big task is to bring the various departmental interests to agreement. It is also found that each plan when put into operation involves social changes within the company which produce unforeseen secondary effects.

It is generally recognised that actual planning work must be done by a project team, but in many companies the initiative comes directly from the top management and in some they play a direct part in the planning process. Business planning is, of course, based on research and the more comprehensive and long-term the planning, the more important research becomes. Production, marketing, even personnel and social factors must be investigated. Yet Japanese companies' research efforts are generally rated relatively low.

Perhaps it is this past neglect that has made the need for research so urgent now. In some instances research has become a status symbol so that a major company can hardly afford to go without heavy expenditure on it. Thus nothing is ever said about the productivity of research centres, some of which are very lavishly equipped and of impressive size. Expenditure in this direction has increased steadily in recent years, some companies spending up to 10% of their sales income on research and development. Even in relatively small companies the cost may be considerable. For example, the Sanyo Chemical Industry Company has 150 of its 600 employees engaged on research on which about 3·5% of the sales proceeds are spent every year. Masatoshi Yoshimura, president of Sanyo, says, 'Of all company problems, there is none more important than the development of creativity. No company can expect to progress or make profits of any size as long as it imitates the methods of others'. Most Japanese managements agree with this view. Research projects are concentrated on the development of new products, the improvement of existing products and marketing, with most researchers' efforts concentrated on technical and scientific problems.

In most companies top management controls both the subject and the frequency of reporting on research progress, attaching particular importance to the manner in which results are communicated to the development and production sections. But no specific information could be obtained for this study on the actual planning and technical development, using the research results, and it may be assumed that this process embodies the same complex relationships between people as in long-term planning.

One curious feature about Japanese research is the relatively infrequent contact between industry and the universities. Again and again Japanese managements made it clear that such collaboration, which could also serve as practical training for graduates, is the exception rather than the rule. However, in December 1969 the Japanese Federation of Employers Associations proposed that a non-partisan consulting body should be set up to promote joint research projects and to examine the possibility of setting up more research universities.

CHAPTER 8

Marketing

It is obvious that the extraordinary growth of production in Japanese industry is closely linked to successful marketing. Forms of organisation and management practices required for this marketing differ considerably from those of European firms. For example, many Japanese companies sell through an independent sales company which frequently works for a larger group.

The large independent trade associations which were originally set up for marketing are a special feature of Japanese business life and their influence is widespread. In 1969, 70·6% of exports and 82·2% of imports were transacted by trade associations with the 10 largest handling at least 50% of exports and 60% of all import business.

To understand the full significance of this system one must be able to visualise the interaction between trade association, financing bank and industrial group. The largest trading association is Mitsubishi Shoji Kaisha with a turnover of $10,000 million in 1970. It controls 12% of Japan's imports and 10% of exports. Its activities are closely connected with the Mitsubishi Bank and the Mitsubishi group of companies.

The tremendous importance of these companies in the export trade is matched by their similar position in domestic business, through the large supermarkets and commercial groups. Thus a very deep division between production and marketing management is typical of many major

Japanese companies. There are, of course, cases where companies have developed their own export departments. Komatsu Manufacturing Ltd. did so in 1955, an unusual step at that time. Initially only two or three people worked on exports, but by 1960 there was a major breakthrough in international markets and by 1964 the export department employed 150 people. Customer service departments were also set up abroad and Komatsu succeeded in building up its export turnover to $67 million a year by 1969.

The concentration of marketing in a few large companies led to the development of very modern management and decision-taking aids. In Tokyo, Mitsui & Co. installed a computer system to connect all foreign-trading client firms, via terminals. This system was already in use for inland branches. Undoubtedly it facilitates the rapid development of export-import business.

Trading companies and associations also act as raw material suppliers and are becoming increasingly active in development businesses such as C. Itoh and Nissho-Iwai, who, with Japanese steel companies are developing an iron ore mine in Liberia, where they all participate together with an American mining company. Similar plans are being made for the petroleum industry in Indonesia by Mitsubishi Shomi, Mitsui & Co. and Sumito.

In inland trade too, the trading associations were the pioneers of large-scale marketing, applying their overseas skills and resources to regional development. The growth of modern industrial estates and of the 'training industry' owe much to these trading houses.

The marketing arm of Japanese large-scale industry is therefore a very powerful organisation, as a direct result of this heavy concentration and of the extraordinarily close association with banks and manufacturing companies. It is not surprising, therefore, to find that marketing managers are given considerable freedom in making their decisions and have a remarkable degree of independence compared to production managers. Whereas in Europe sales promotion is designed and carried out in discussion with the traditionally influential heads of production in the same company, Japanese competitors in world markets operate in a quite different dimension.

CHAPTER 9

Personnel Policy and Practice

As a result of the extraordinary and far reaching changes which have taken place in Japanese production and marketing methods, there has had to be a major switch from pure personnel administration to a comprehensive policy on long-term personnel planning. Considerable progress has been made in this direction by most of the major firms. As with European businesses, such a change presents special problems for any personnel planning department. Not least is the adaption of the numbers and the quality of labour to business requirements. In spite of the Japanese system of permanent employment (shushin koyo) and the seniority principle (nenko jeretsu) still in widespread use, both of which set limits to the degree of adaption, most companies have succeeded in keeping their personnel practices relatively flexible.

What are the possibilities, within these limitations, of changing the labour force radically to meet changing requirements? Firstly, internal transfers predominated until 1965. But with the expansion of companies and their merging into bigger groups, transfers to other firms became normal practice. In such transfers previous wage rates, social security benefits and seniority status are maintained.

Second, premature retirement. This method was employed in the fertilizer industry between 1962 and early 1964 when 10% to 15% of the staff were released. An attempt was made to restrict the numbers involved by selecting those nearing the normal age limit and also the less efficient people. They were given financial support as well as assistance in finding new employment.

A company's recruitment policy is most important for the development of the desired personnel structure. Recruits to major Japanese companies are largely school leavers and college graduates, and since promotion is closely linked with the level of education attained and the quality of the educational institution attended, there is extraordinarily strong competition for admission to the upper secondary schools and colleges. As a result, by March 1970 the number of university graduates entering working life was for the first time greater than the number of lower secondary school leavers.

At one time efforts were made to improve the quality of personnel, particularly for the higher positions, by employing only graduates from certain key universities, in some cases from only one or two. However, the serious shortage of school leavers has made recruitment practices considerably more flexible. There is now recruitment from a large number of universities with a recognised standard of performance.

Employment policy in Japanese large-scale industry involves the evaluation of applicants according to their learning ability, ability to work together and their health. To this end special entry examinations are held, supplemented by group discussions and by a thorough medical examination. Curiously enough, job applicants do not normally have any technical training. General education has a clear priority. No career-orientated instruction is given during the compulsory school years. True, in 1968 career instruction began in the top classes of the upper secondary schools but this was attended by only 35% of the pupils, and even this teaching provided only elementary background knowledge.

By comparison with the highly developed apprentice-ship systems in Europe and the U.S.A., the general education system might seem to place the Japanese at a disadvantage. But experience in Japan shows that young workers with no special career training do not necessarily impede industrial development. On the contrary, it could be argued that the potential adaptability of labour with a suitable general education has contributed to the growth of Japanese industry.

An individual's chances of employment depend both on his education and on the results of his potential employer's tests. In many cases a year's trial, followed by a further selection process, are agreed upon before the applicant becomes a member of the 'permanent staff'. Without doubt the relatively high level of general education and also the very low average age of Japanese workers (most girls and women work only until they marry) contribute to the remarkable ability of Japanese employees to adapt to whatever work is required of them.

CHAPTER 10

The Wages System

The wages system in Japanese heavy industry can only be understood in terms of the principle of permanent employment. Unlike European practice where wage and salary rates are related closely to work value or output, the main feature of Japanese industrial wages policy is the relationship between wage or salary level and length of service with the firm. There are many time-based systems of redistribution of the total wage and salary bill, in the form of bonus payments.

This specifically Japanese wages system is the result of an historical development. When industrialisation began in the Meiji period, 1868–1911, the idea of efficiency wages prevailed. During the Taisho period, 1912–1925 this was replaced by wages based on length of service, in order to promote a closer union between company and workers. During the Second World War the necessity for employing large numbers of uneducated workers meant that payment had to be largely a 'social wage' based on family size and its requirements.

Even in the post-war period, with its pressure of inflation, this social concept was given considerable support by the trade unions who fought for a system of wages based on the minimum living standards that they aimed at. However, in the Japanese context of permanent employment, this resulted in the development of a system which allowed annual increments based on length of service.

In 1950 several companies began to introduce work value wages on the pattern of American experience. But it was soon apparent that the Western work value system could not yet be applied in Japanese industry without considerable adaptation. In most advanced industrial companies, the present wage structure is a compromise between these two concepts.

It is customary in Japanese industry to make wage or salary payments monthly. College graduates receive fixed monthly salaries, but upper and lower secondary school leavers initially receive payments calculated on daily or hourly rates, less deductions for, among other things, failure to keep to fixed work times. If, however, a worker is absent and has a good reason, then within certain limits full wages are paid. Workers are classified either as monthly wage or monthly salary earners, each group having a basic rate. The significance of the basic rate is that it forms the base for calculating pensions and a range of additional remunerations. Incentive bonuses are very small in proportion to total earnings although in the steel industry attempts are being made to increase this percentage to as much as 35%.

In contrast to European bonus systems most Japanese firms invariably take into account length of service, which serves as the yardstick, before superimposing payments based on ability. As in Europe, output bonuses are paid mainly to production and shop floor workers, office staff receiving extra payments related to various efficiency measurements.

Again, in common with Europe, cost of living bonuses are meant to compensate for price rises, but they differ in that they are paid primarily on the basis of family size, regional differences in living costs, commuter expenditure and as an allowance for rent. In addition to these regular wage components there is, of course, pay for overtime, the maximum allowed being agreed between managements and trade unions.

Generally speaking, all permanently employed workers

receive large bonuses in July and December, depending on the financial position of the company, and these usually amount to between three and six months' salary. Basically these are withheld wages which on the one hand enable the employee to make 'once-for-all' purchases of expensive household items but on the other hand, give to a company some flexible control over wage costs.

Housing costs are closely related to wage costs in Japanese companies. About 40% of the workers live in company-owned accommodation although many firms make loans available for acquiring dwellings or they run their own housing associations.

Leisure programmes also come within the framework of voluntary social costs borne by companies with so-called health centres playing an important part in the recreational facilities provided. As one steel company executive states: '63% of our workers wake up every morning in a company-owned house or flat. Almost all public transport costs to and from their places of work are reimbursed to them. All hospital services are free, cheap meals are served in the works canteens and company-owned supermarkets provide almost all household goods at low prices. A worker can play tennis on a company-owned court, have his hair cut at the company-owned hairdresser's, a beer at the company-owned club and go to a public swimming bath which is also run by the firm. At the weekend he can take his family and stay overnight in a company-owned recreation centre in the mountains'.

Clearly the Japanese permanent employee finds his most important material requirements satisfied by his company and he is spared the exercise of his own initiative.

Salaries of managerial employees are not subject to group negotiation. The basic structure is the same as that of other workers, salaries increasing with length of service and bonus payments being calculated on this basis. As in Europe, the directors are not paid a salary for their directorial services, as such, but contrary to European practice, the directors are normally over the customary pensionable age. As we have already seen, however, pensionable age is low.

In addition to their salaries and cash bonuses, top managerial staff receive company share bonuses by way of extra, thus putting their total remuneration far above middle management levels. They also receive numerous fringe benefits—company cars, company-owned houses, membership of exclusive clubs and large untaxed expense accounts.

An expense account plays an extremely important part as a status symbol, enabling managers to participate in demonstrative activities—dining out, playing golf, etc. But it must be borne in mind that, like the European business-man's luncheon, a large part of Japanese business life takes place unofficially at exclusive bars and clubs in the evenings and therefore it can be claimed that such activities are in the interests of business.

CHAPTER 11

Training and Methods of Promotion

In the management of Japanese large-scale industry, methods of training and promoting staff occupy an important position. This is because, as stated earlier, new recruits are employed without any particular career training. Industry concentrates on intensive education and training programmes, not on career development but on functional ability. Thus a report by the Japan Iron & Steel Federation begins, 'As a result of the qualitative changes in work requirements, during the course of technical progress, the former methods of obtaining skilled workers have become out-dated. It is now considered more important to have a systematic plan for instructing those production workers who have to operate complex machines efficiently and intelligently'.

Around 1960 the major companies set up training departments which gradually grew into large units. Training was comprehensive and intensive, since the career qualifications of every trainee depended on this. Of utmost importance was the training of newly-recruited production workers and office employees and also the further education of middle management. Further education outside the company was also made possible.

As part of the training, orientation courses for new recruits were often continued in group discussions and even after work, in the dormitories. Group thought and group consciousness dominate Japanese working life and there are numerous activities to support the integration of new workers.

Today in the Japanese iron and steel industry, where training schemes are well advanced, there are over 20 companies which run three-year apprentice training courses. However, the conventional system of apprentice training for school leavers is disappearing with the growing need for professional skills, as the iron and steel industry adopts more advanced technical methods of production.

In addition, school leavers become fewer as more young people stay on to college, for further education. In 1961 31 companies were training 3,767 apprentices from lower secondary schools. By 1969 the number of companies giving such training had fallen to 18 and the number of trainees to 2,195. The old system was giving way to a tendency to employ upper secondary school leavers as production workers. Their industrial training consists of a short introductory course followed by training at the place of work. This seems to be sufficient for the simpler areas of operation but considerable expert knowledge and technical skill are expected from maintenance personnel. For this reason some companies hold day-release courses for this group of workers which extend over 1 to $1\frac{1}{2}$ years, immediately after recruitment. Subjects covered include mechanical engineering, electrical theory, measurement and control methods. New recruits are also made familiar with, among other subjects, modern management techniques such as quality control, operations research and electronic data processing.

Later, those employed in technical areas receive training as technicians or technical engineers. Companies run two-year courses in subjects ranging through metallurgy, metal processing, mechanical, electrical and chemical engineering.

As with workshop employees, newly-recruited office staff undergo training. The aim is to impart a general knowledge of the industry, its production processes, the history and structure of the company. Particular attention is devoted to the training of college and university graduates for managerial posts and for staff positions requiring high qualifications.

Non-technical office staff are also trained for their jobs and the sales staff in particular are given a grounding in product knowledge, sales techniques and the basic technology of the products. In recent years the dissemination of knowledge on electronic data processing and computer technology has become extremely important.

All the major companies visited by the author pay particular attention to the training and further training of middle management. Usually workers who are selected as potential foremen (kocho) attend courses varying from 4 or 5 days to one month. In the iron and steel industry there is a full-time course lasting 6 months. After appointment to foreman, refresher courses lasting 4 or 5 days are repeated from time to time. They deal with the economic, technical and in particular the human problems of the workshop. An example of the schedule for a foremen's refresher course is given in the following table.

Schedule of a Short Course for Foremen

	7	8	9	10	11	12	13	14	15	16	17	18	19	20	21	22	Hours
Day 1	Breakfast	Break / Gymnastics	Meeting at the Iron & Steel Junior College			Opening speech / Explanations	Introduction of participants		Lecture 'Developing trends in the iron and steel industry'			Break	Evening meal		Free discussion		
Day 2	Breakfast	Break / Gymnastics	Lecture: 'How technical capacity is controlled'		Break	Lunch	Break	Group discussion: 'Work control'			Break		Evening meal		Free discussion		
Day 3	Breakfast	Break / Gymnastics	Discussion: 'Work control'		Break	Lecture: 'Management'		Lunch	Group discussion: 'Worker control'		Break		Evening meal		Free discussion		
Day 4	Breakfast	Break / Gymnastics	Discussion: 'Worker control'		Break	Training in self evaluation		Lunch	Inspection of the Iron & Steel Junior College		Training in self evaluation			Retrospective view of seminar	Social event	Free	
Day 5	Breakfast / Departure 7.00		Arrival 9.00 / Inspection o the Hirobata Company / Introduction / Works visit			Question time		Discussion with the company manager			Parting speech						

CHAPTER 12

Managerial Training

Further education courses for departmental managers are arranged in some form or other by all the major Japanese companies. Their purpose differs little from those of similar courses in Europe. Essentially they deal with management techniques, leadership and the solution of administrative problems. The methods used compare well with international standards. Group-based further education is given at residential courses lasting from 2 days to a week. The table that follows gives an example of the programme for such a residential course.

A peculiarity of Japanese companies, with regard to the promotion of middle management, is the large number of study trips abroad, generally in groups. Considerable sums of money are spent on these trips by the companies who also provide opportunities for educational holidays abroad for independent study and many of the larger companies arrange for studies to be finished abroad.

Systematic management training in the strict sense of the word is not practised in Japanese large-scale industry. There are indeed a number of lectures, discussions and study trips, but more comprehensive management courses are mainly held outside these big companies. Employers' associations arrange courses, conferences and seminars which are sometimes spectacular. For instance, Nikkeiren, the Japanese Association of Employers' Unions, arranged a two-weeks cruise in November 1970 as part of a further education course, on board a 14,000-ton vessel which called at Hong Kong, Taiwan and Okinawa. The cruise was

Schedule of a Short Course for Departmental Managers

	9.00	10.00	11.00	12.00	13.00 14.00 15.00	16.00	17.00	18.00 19.00
Day 1	Opening speeches	Introduction of the participants	Discussion: Duties of the departmental	Lunch	Lecture: 'Progress in world business and Japan'	Discussion group	Discussion group	Evening meal
Day 2	Discussion circle	Discussion: Duties of the departmental manager 'The development of correct employer-employee relations'		Lunch	Discussion group	Discussion group	Discussion group	Evening meal
Day 3	Discussion circle	Lecture: 'Human problems in business management'		Lunch	Lecture: 'Long-term planning in the iron and steel industry and our company'	Discussion group		Evening meal
Day 4	Lecture: 'Basic questions in business management and administration'			Lunch	discussion group	Discussion group	Lecture by Social vice president	evening
Day 5	Discussion circle	Discussion circle		Lecture by Vice president	Discussion: Duties of the departmental manager: 'Worker control'	Conclusion		Departure

attended by 480 foremen from 221 companies. It was a fitting conclusion to general foreman training and emphasised the importance that management attaches to broadening the mental horizon of these employees.

It is evident from the study made of the advanced training system in Japanese large-scale industry, that this training is considered to be of great importance in the choice of suitable personnel for promotion. However, there is hardly any sign of systematic career planning, on the basis of co-operation between the personnel and training departments and the employee's immediate superior. But there are so-called career development programmes, such as the one at Showa Denko, which seek to establish systematically the promotion conditions for suitable candidates.

Promotions based on length of service and certain traditional qualities of character are very rarely encountered today. Operating performance is gaining increasing weight as a promotion factor and so also are training and further training.

In large-scale industry a minimum period of service is stipulated for promotion to the next grade and only in exceptional circumstances can this period be shortened. Thus a university graduate, for instance, cannot be promoted to group manager until he has completed 7 to 10 years' service. To become a department manager the minimum period is 10 to 15 years while promotion to chief department manager is rare in less than 20 years. The Japanese executive must therefore work his way up over a long period. There is no such thing as a lightning career.

The method common in Western countries of accelerating a career by changing companies is impossible in Japan. Employees usually remain tied to an employer until retirement and when this is not possible, any change of company must be explained and fully justified. Managerial staff are recruited from outside only in exceptional circumstances, as when experts are needed in banking or with inside knowledge of public administration. There are, of course, possibilities for promotion by moving to a newly-formed subsidiary or a jointly owned company.

Recommendations for promotion are normally put forward by an executive, but the personnel department always tests the candidate. At the lower levels this test takes the form of a school examination in general administration methods. On the result, the chief business manager in the relevant section decides. Promotion to departmental manager and above is generally decided by the president of the company or by a director.

The table below indicates the general requirements expected of an executive if he is to make good decisions, in the view of the sample of managers interviewed for this study.

Executive qualifications

1.	Far-sightedness	64·8%
2.	Capacity to handle people	10·1%
3.	Specialist knowledge	3·6%
4.	Knowledge of the interrelationship between departments	2·4%
5.	Training unnecessary	3·5%
6.	Other replies	2·3%
7.	No reply	13·3%
		100·0%

If far-sightedness is concerned with understanding what people are likely to want to buy tomorrow, then it is obvious from the table that personality factors are considered to be particularly important in Japanese management while purely specialist knowledge is placed in the background. This also recognises that an executive's job is to bring about efficient work and co-operation between all employees. Functional and personal authority are, however, intermixed in the Japanese executive structure and accordingly the promotion criteria for potential management are both technically and socially oriented.

CHAPTER 13

Worker Participation

Japanese business management is reputed to be extremely paternalistic. This view is, however, misleading, as not even in the past was there very much of a leader-follower mentality made humanly bearable by comprehensive welfare measures. On the contrary, authoritarian distribution of power was tolerated because there was a strong sense of mutual obligation and a common interest in the good of the company, also because each worker looked on the company as his home.

With the modernisation of the economic and social structure, Japanese management, at least in large-scale industry, was faced with the problem of gradually transforming the social organisation of their companies by improving the opportunities for participation by all their workers. The most important driving forces in this direction, besides the persistent demand from the workers, as made more effective by the shortage of labour, were and are today undoubtedly the soul-destroying, alienating phenomena in a highly rationalised but not yet fully automated business.

Three principal starting points may be used by Japanese company management for broadening the basis of participation by their employees. The first has for long been a tradition of the Western industrialised countries: participation of employee representatives in joint consultation with management. There are similar joint councils in many Japanese companies.

A study by the Japanese Productivity Centre in 1968

showed that the most widely mentioned objectives of works councils or committees were the improvement of understanding and the harmonious running of the business. Next in importance came higher productivity and efficiency. Bottom of the list came these four worker-oriented subjects—improvement of working conditions, implementation of collective bargaining, avoidance of disputes and dealing with grievances.

Participation in a works council does not, however, involve employees' representatives in the actual planning process but in contact with management after they have put forward their proposals. Participation is essentially limited to rights relating to information supplied and proposals presented.

A realistic picture of these committee methods is provided by this report of a major company: 'To achieve a closer contact between management and trade union, we have introduced a committee known as a 'management council' composed of representatives of the employers and of the trade union. This committee meets at the beginning of each year to hear the president and various members of the management describe the company's policy and plans for the ensuing year and to discuss them. At other meetings of this committee, held regularly every three months, the production schedule, the marketing plan and the interim reports on these activities are presented. This gives the trade union a full understanding of the company's policy and makes teamwork easier. These efforts have probably contributed greatly towards the fact that we have never had any unnecessary friction between management and union and we have worked together to achieve our common goal of higher productivity. In these days of rapid change in world conditions, we believe "management councils" are very valuable in the successful execution of our business.'

A second possibility of promoting worker participation is offered by Japanese management in their attempts at reconstruction of company organisation. This largely concerns de-centralisation measures which so far have not noticeably altered the inflexible executive order. But initiatives in this direction are gaining increasing sympathy and are being imitated.

Finally, the third point: changes in style of management. An attempt by Sony and Kawasaki-Steel in particular, to form autonomous working groups with fewer than 20 workers, must be mentioned. The leaders of these groups themselves form small groups so that a new and parallel company management is built up on this basis.

What is important, however, is the attempt to get these leaders or 'speakers' informally elected and then to have their duties ratified by the management.

The creation of informal opportunities, on a group basis, appears to have met with considerable success and the idea of general participation has become the principal philosophy of some managers. It is significant that Takao Nagata, president of Hitachi Shipbuilding and Engineering Co., speaking on employer/employee relations in Japanese industry, has stated: 'My management philosophy and my sincere desire lead me to advocate the energetic promotion, in the hectic 70s, of a type of management in which everyone takes part'.

A survey of personnel policies and trends in Japanese large-scale industry should end with a reference to those problem areas which are uppermost in the minds of the parties concerned. It is remarkable how much the traditional principles of Japanese personnel management are subjected to pressure for change. The principles of permanent employment, worker evaluation according to length of service and compulsory early retirement have come under question.

The need for promoting and using the efficiency potential of workers by better motivation and better training is being increasingly recognized. However, this is regarded essentially as a managerial task, something which must be done *for* the workers and which in some cases must also be achieved jointly *with* them.

The solution of some of these tasks *by* the workers is regarded as essentially an improved performance of functions delegated by management. Yet the tendency to increasing participation by employees indicates a permanent revision of traditional viewpoints of authority.

CHAPTER 14

Criteria for Success

The relationships between business success, management structure and managerial behaviour have been examined for Japanese large-scale industry by Toyohiro Kono, professor at the Gakushuin University in Tokyo. He made a close study of 50 fast-growth companies for the period from 1955 to 1965, but his analysis of the factors relevant to success is based on a comparison of 47 of these fast-growth firms, whose turnovers had risen in those 10 years by an average of 6·9 times, with 29 firms which showed only a doubling of their turnovers. In 1955 the profit margins of both groups were approximately the same. During the 10-year period the general trend was downward but this was more obvious in the slower growth companies. The fast-growth firms had greater opportunities for self-financing, to increase their capital.

Companies in the latter group owe their progress to a dynamic goal concept, based on company research, product development and co-operation with other firms, particularly in marketing. In this way, competitive pressure on prices is reduced or postponed by the introduction of new products. Professor Kono believes that market penetration through the introduction of new products, and in this way attracting high, uncompetitive profits, is particularly important for the success of a company.

Regarding the differences in organisation structure, Professor Kono emphasises the trend towards collective decision-making, thorough planning and flexibility of the organisation structure in fast-growth companies. The slow-growth firms are much more static in organisation. He also compares management methods, finds a better inter-departmental flow of information in the first group and their managements are prepared to take greater risks. Professor Kono's study evaluates the success factors of Japanese companies during a period of rapid economic growth. In the present phase of consolidation financed by recent growth profits, re-grouping into market sectors and rationalisation of product lines, new management strategies are necessary.

Growth profits cannot be achieved by developing new production facilities, since these are already up to the capacity required. Neither can any noticeable improvement be expected from the fuller use of the available equipment. Consequently, organisational flexibility and the adaptability of management and its workers, to meet changing market requirements, are becoming the central problem. In this respect Japanese industry is following the trend now evident in all highly developed industrial countries.

CHAPTER 15

The Companies Involved

To provide a broad base for this survey of management systems and practices in large-scale Japanese industry, a personally conducted research effort was mounted in eight companies. They were two steel producers, Nippon Steel Corporation and Sumitomo Metal Industries Ltd., one motor manufacturer, Toyoto Motor Co. Ltd., two chemical companies, Mitsubishi Chemical Industries Ltd. and Showa Denko Ltd., one industrial plant construction firm, Chiyoda Chemical Engineering and Construction Co. Ltd., and two major companies in the electrical industry, Mitsubishi Electric Corporation and Tokyo Shinaura Electric Co. Ltd. In all these companies detailed discussions were held with members of top management and with expert staff from personnel departments.

Nippon Steel Corporation, the leading steel company, came into being in 1970 as a result of the merger of Yawata Iron and Steel and Fuji Iron and Steel. Both had been members of the State Japan Iron and Steel Company from 1934 to 1950. Nippon Steel has a capital of 229,360 million yen and in the Japanese financial year of 1969 produced 31 million tons of crude steel at its 10 plants. It accounted for 38% of Japan's total steel exports. A new plant at Oita, on Kyushu island has been built to produce 7·5 million tons of crude steel annually from the middle of 1972. In July 1970 the company had 83,859 workpeople and its top management team consisted of 43 people.

The chairman of the board and the president have six vice presidents assisting them, who represent clearly defined specialist fields: planning and finance, subsidiary companies, general administration, buildings and plant, sales, production and research, and the management of the plants at Yawata. Untypical of Japanese companies, the six vice presidents, the 14 general managers and 11 other directors also have clearly defined market areas for which they are personally responsible.

Selection of Nippon's managerial staff is based on qualifications, operating performance and personality as evaluated unanimously by the directors. There is no automatic promotion to top managerial positions, according to length of service. Nor is educational background of over-riding significance. The general manager responsible for finance had only a lower secondary school education. Promotion of managerial staff is dependent on their knowledge, planning ability and creativity. The idea of 'management by objectives' is not formally put into practice, but it serves as a guiding principle.

There is no systematic career planning in the Nippon Steel Corporation. No advance decisions are made on employees' careers. No psychologists participate in the selection of personnel. It appears that managers themselves are expected to apply psychological knowledge.

Training for middle management emphasises the practical application of knowledge as opposed to the pure communication of knowledge. International experience is regarded highly and workers are encouraged to travel abroad as often as possible.

In the 'lower management' bracket, Nippon Steel has introduced the American foreman system. Each foreman has to supervise an average of three overseers (kocho), who themselves have 10 to 15 workers under them. The foremen are generally selected from these overseers for their outstanding work and managerial qualities. All workers in the Nippon Steel Corporation have staff status and can be promoted to supervisory and management positions.

Sumitomo Metal Industries. This company, belonging to the Sumitomo group, was founded in 1897. It's production capacity is over 10 million tons of crude steel a year and it also has a modern plant for the manufacture of finished products. It has five main works and its production has increased tenfold in the last 10 years. In 1969 exports totalled 30·6% of output.

In 1970 Sumitomo Metal Industries had a labour force of 32,414, with a top management which included 29 directors all over the age of 50, of whom 28 were university graduates. Decision-making methods vary according to the degree of urgency, with quick decisions being made by top management in a verbal statement. In all other cases the ringi system is used with departmental managers meeting twice a month at a working lunch and also having informal talks, generally in the evenings at a club. General administrative information is presented in the works' magazine once a month and general announcements are posted around the plants.

Middle management includes 148 chief departmental managers, 135 acting chief departmental managers and 408 departmental managers. Their average age is 46 and about half of them consist of university and college graduates. Management training is given within the firm. Training of 'workers' follows the pattern outlined in earlier chapters, with school leavers completing very intensive orientation and practical courses, and being encouraged to take part in planning and detailed plan preparation. The American foreman system was introduced five years ago and there are apprenticeships on the European pattern.

Toyoto Motor Co. This firm was founded in 1937 and all production plants are concentrated in Toyoto City, a typical Japanese 'company town'. In 1969, 964,000 passenger vehicles, 468,000 lorries and 39,000 special vehicles were manufactured in the five production shops. With 31·5% of

Japan's total vehicle production in 1969 the company is the biggest manufacturer of automobiles in the country. It has 11 subsidiaries and 259 supply firms are closely linked with it. Although Toyoto Sales Company was formed to market the vehicles, sales are transacted through independent dealers, 251 in Japan and 142 overseas, whose capital equipment is partly paid for by the company. There are also 14 overseas assembly plants catering for 20% of the cars exported. The company employs 38,500 workers and has an upper management of 19 directors, 16 of whom are responsible for special departments or functions.

Decision-making in the top management group has a dual structure. The ringi system is used only in certain types of situations, such as contracts, court cases, purchase of buildings and land and investments of over 10 million yen. Fundamental decisions regarding business policy, and therefore concerning the development and manufacture of new products, are taken by a special committee headed by a chief general manager and including other directors. There are about 100 chief departmental managers and acting chief departmental managers, 200 departmental managers and about 500 group managers. The latter group includes 300 foremen who supervise about 100 workers each. Commercial and technical staff are about 50% university graduates.

The Toyoto Motor Company's training system merits particular attention. At Toyoto City a technical high school, run by the company, is attended by 1,500 students between the ages of 15 and 18. Inside the company there is a highly developed system of worker promotion based on (1) Contribution to creativity. (2) A positive attitude towards the company and (3) the fostering of a company consciousness. All of this adds up to much the same system as in other firms but is probably more intense in Toyoto. The relatively intense worker production rate in the Toyoto Motor Company probably results from the fact that the average age of the firm's employees is below that in other large companies.

Mitsubishi Chemical Industries. This company forms part of the Mitsubishi group, the oldest part of which was founded in 1870. The group embraces 40 large companies employing 323,000 workers and having a turnover of 213 million yen. There are 24 subsidiary companies and supply firms.

The board of directors of Mitsubishi Chemical Industries consists of 27 executives. The president of the company is a lawyer by background, one of the vice-presidents is also a lawyer and the other a chemist. Top management consists of two groups, one group being staff specialists and the other being line management, divided into seven divisions representing the various product groups. An attempt has recently been made to draw up a five-year development plan for the company and a special staff department has been set up for this purpose.

University graduates and high school or college graduates predominate in middle management. Lower managerial appointments are made according to efficiency and suitability for a particular function. In this company, particular attention is given to the responsibility of managerial staff not only to allocate jobs but also to promote talent.

Showa Denko. This is one of the largest Japanese companies engaged in electro-chemistry, with particular emphasis on petrochemical products and on aluminium production. It dates back to 1908 when Sobo Marine Products was set up to produce iodine and calcium chloride. The existing company was formed from a merger with Showa Fertiliser in 1939 and has 11 production centres. The company consumes more electricity than any other private enterprise in Japan, but generates 30% of its requirements at its own power stations. In 1970 turnover was valued at 154·3 milliard yen. There are 32 subsidiary companies and in some cases these also form joint firms with other companies such as Dupont, Philips Petroleum or Sumitomo Chemical.

Top management consists of 27 executives, with a president, vice-president, two chief general managers, six general managers and 14 directors. Their average age is about 55. Appointments to the board are made from within the company. Only one chief general manager has been engaged from outside the company before being appointed to the board. Evolution of the basic rules for top managerial decisions has been influenced by three systems: the works council system, discussed earlier; the Showa-Denko long range planning system (SLORPS) which embodies a financial plan, a sales plan and a project evaluation system; also the ringi system, which at Showa Denko has only limited significance since top management generally takes the initiative on matters of decision.

The company has introduced a self-evaluation system. A questionnaire is issued every year to be completed by all staff from assistant foreman to acting chief departmental manager. From this, as explained earlier, it can be ascertained where, at what and on the basis of what knowledge a worker would like to be employed.

Chiyoda Chemical Engineering and Construction, which is engaged essentially in the planning and establishment of industrial plants for the chemical industry, was founded in 1948. Recent major projects completed include petroleum refineries in Japan, in Southern Asia and in the Near East and plants for production of butyl rubber, ethylene and ordinary paraffin. Chiyoda Chemical employs 2,700 workers, of which 1,500 are engineers and technicians. The board of directors consists of 23 executives and includes 10 university graduates who are neither engineers nor chemists.

Staff are divided into the traditional categories of administration, research, design and production. For every plant project, a team headed by an experienced project manager is set up, and this team is then solely responsible for the project. Where necessary, for the setting up of new plants overseas, workers are given special training. There are courses in the language of the country itself and an introduction to the conventions of the country. The men who were to work in Saudi Arabia were sent to the University of Cairo for a three-year course.

A peculiarity of personnel management at Chiyoda is that an employee may retire at his own request at the age of 42. Workers who stay on may either continue working without further increases in pay up to the age of 55 or may 'negotiate' pay increases every 2 years. In most Japanese companies a worker is unable to negotiate the conditions of his working contract.

Mitsubishi Electric Corporation. This company, a member of the Mitsubishi group, was established in 1906. In 1921 it was registered as an independent company and now employs 55,000 workers at 19 production plants. The board of directors consists of 28 executives, all of whom are university graduates. Important decisions are taken either at meetings of the general management committee or within the top management of each division. The ringi system is used occasionally.

Management training and promotion broadly follow the same lines as in most large-scale companies. One exception is that personnel policy is centralised. Every departmental manager is responsible for his own staff but all general staff problems are settled on a central basis. Like Showa Denko, in the electro-chemical industry, Mitsubishi Electric has links with the U.S.A. through a 'knowhow' exchange scheme with Westinghouse Electric.

Tokyo Shibaura Electric (Toshiba). This large company in the electrical industry, founded in 1875, has a turnover of about 600 milliard yen. In July 1970 84,500 employees were engaged at 24 factories. Its Tsurumi plant at Yokohama is Asia's largest for the assembly of heavy electrical installations. At its Osaka factory 50,000 washing machines leave the conveyor belt every month and its central research laboratory, with over 1,100 scientists, is Asia's largest private research institution. The board of directors consists of 26 executives and its organisation structure follows Japanese general procedure except that the ringi system is not used. However, whereas in other firms the president always takes the decisions by signing documents in his own room alone, at Toshiba this is done in the presence of all the directors. The company maintains the usual three Japanese management levels, top, middle and lower. There are about 1,100 departmental managers and about 2,500 group managers. The position of group manager was introduced in 1970, to coordinate the work of staff and line managers at the place of work. Transfer of employees from factory to office is very common and there is no difference in the treatment of workers and staff.

At Toshiba retirement conditions differ from those at most other companies. Compulsory retirement for men is at age 56 but it is possible to continue in employment until the age of 60 at, initially, 95% of salary. This is reduced by 10% each successive year, but can be raised in line with general salary increases.

CHAPTER 16

Summary of Findings

Each of the eight companies we have been discussing occupies the top position in its own business field and all are characterised by having had a continuous period of extraordinary growth. Thus it can fairly be said that we are dealing with the most advanced sections of Japanese industry.

With one exception, top management is recognised as the board of directors. Only at Toshiba are the chief departmental managers also included. The organisation principles of the companies vary considerably, but division into staff and line departments, and in the latter again into product groups, is predominant. A special form of this is found at Chiyoda Chemical Engineering where matrix management, organisation into project groups, has been put into action.

Decision-making processes on the boards of directors are varied, with strict application of the ringi system the exception rather than the rule. Generally the most important decisions are made by the president, the vice-presidents and the chief managers.

The ringi system appears to play a more important part in the communciation of top management with the lower levels. Here also the conference method is used, but often the conferences consist essentially of managerial speeches without opportunities for discussion. It is evident that work is now being done on the development of modern information systems.

Education of company management is at an extraordinarily high level throughout. Non-academics are the exception, being mostly older staff whose opportunities for further education were limited in their youth. There is no clear preponderance of technicians and scientists over economists and lawyers and other specialists. Careers in the company are the rule, the employment of managerial staff from outside the company being exceptional.

Middle management shows a distinct preponderance of over 40s and top appointments in the over 55 age group are rarely made, since retirement is compulsory on reaching 55 or 56. As mentioned earlier, the retirees are usually allowed to continue work, but under different conditions.

Even in lower management the average age is still relatively high, as is the length of service. This is due to the great importance which is still attached to the principle of seniority in promotions. The level of education also is remarkable in this management group, an overwhelming majority having had a university education. Of course, there are opportunities for high school graduates to be promoted to lower management and the number who have risen from production work is in some cases extremely high. The tendency to apply the American foreman system in the works is very noticeable, while in several cases the German chief foreman system has also had a considerable influence on works methods. In all the companies investigated, the recruitment processes were carried out with great care, strict selection methods being used, applying psychological tests, both general and specific to the work role required. Trial employment on probation is not uncommon either. It is particularly practised by the Toyota Motor Company.

To obtain satisfactory recruits some of the companies award university scholarships and those who receive them are not required to pay back the monetary grants on joining the company. Although in Japan it is widely thought that when employing university graduates preference should be given to certain universities, each of the companies, with the exception of Mitsubishi Chemical, did in fact consider most universities when seeking suitable potential employees.

It is interesting to note that only at Showa Denko is personnel planning based on both a self-evaluation form and evaluation by a superior. Obviously great importance is attached to the promotion of production workers by all the companies, but the methods used are socio-psychological and socio-pedagogical, and are supplementary to the purely technical requirement, most of which is provided by further education while working for the company. Study trips abroad are considered to be extremely important, particularly in view of the isolated geographical position of Japan.

The basis of labour relations is agreements reached with the appropriate trade union. Company management evidently has considerable leeway in shaping such agreements to individual tastes. Wage increases, for example, are generally negotiated on a global basis and not for each specific group. The individual worker also has in some cases opportunity to negotiate his pay. An example of this is Chiyoda Chemical Engineering.

At best, labour relations in major Japanese companies can perhaps be compared to the relations between company management and works councils in Europe, with the important limitation that the Japanese works trade union has the right to strike but has no rights of co-operation or co-determination, as known in a European company's works council, particularly in Germany.

The classic division into workers and staff (mibun principle) had been formally abandoned in the major companies consulted, but the actual day-to-day working distinctions are often still very difficult to overcome. However, the division of employees into groups with different educational levels is considered very important.

Particularly striking in the analysis of employees of the

eight companies was the high number of unmarried workers. Also, even after allowing for the early retirement age, it was found that the average age of the employee was astonishingly low. The explanation is that the extraordinary growth of the companies in recent years has led to a large influx of young people.

For this reason, personnel policy in major Japanese companies has assumed a unique character. Of particular importance are the problems of job training, education and general training. It is understandable, therefore, that these companies are strongly oriented towards social service, not least expressed in the abundance of their voluntary social contributions.

CHAPTER 17

Management Methods and Policies for Social Change

The development of Japanese industry since the Second World War has been fantastic and unprecedented. Nevertheless a certain continuity in the convictions of Japanese management has been successfully preserved and its internal social relations protected to some degree from possible change.

However, changes of considerable magnitude had to be made by the companies studied, as they adapted themselves to changing world conditions, and the question remains—what are the chances of continuing further development of management methods and practices?

If we look at the possibilities for increasing production, it must be realised that the position is becoming more difficult for Japanese management. Firstly, for raw materials, Japanese large-scale industry depends mainly on imports. In 1969 over 70% of imports were non-industrial goods. More specifically, 35·9% were raw materials. As a result of increases in crude oil prices by the Organisation for Petroleum Exporting Countries (OPEC) energy costs in Japanese large-scale industry have risen sharply. Great efforts must be made to become independent of the world market, at least in some sections of energy supply.

The developing countries are the prime source of raw materials. Difficulties are being experienced, particularly in East and South-east Asia, where the respective governments fear Japanese control of their mineral resources. Unilateral Japanese influence on their sales of raw materials and hence on the profits from them will not be tolerated for long, for political reasons.

As a second important factor determining growth potential, we must consider the problem of capitalisation. Indirect financing of investments is a typical feature of Japanese large-scale industry. The banks give credit to companies whose capital is relatively small, a system of capital acquisition which, initially, has considerable advantages. In addition, the national policy of low interest rates is a contributory factor in keeping the costs of borrowing relatively low.

However, this system of obtaining capital also has adverse effects. A free capital market was developed only after long delays. Consequently, greatly varying interest rates were established for different credit periods which in turn resulted in the misdirection of available credits. More important still were the difficulties placed in the way of a consistently anti-inflationary bank policy. Thus new ways must be found for companies to acquire capital.

The most difficult areas of change are seen in the labour market. Since 1966–67 the proportion of the population employed in industry has actually decreased. Lower birth rate age-groups are now reaching the adult age group, longer school education results in few school leavers, at least temporarily, and finally the quota of middle-aged women engaged in industry is stagnating and some reduction in working hours must be expected. Further, not enough recruits are available for production work, while the supply of labour for office posts is much greater. As the level of education is raised, young people tend to choose non-manual careers, particularly those in the tertiary sector.

The restriction of the labour force in a period of unchecked economic growth was also a reason for considerable wage increases which in 1970 overtook productivity increases. This is producing problems that are completely new to the Japanese companies, for on average in the past few years company profits have far outstripped wage increases. From 1965 to 1970 incomes rose by about 17% per annum while company profits rose by more than 27%.

An important factor affecting production is the extraordinary shortage of space in the industrial centres. The building of new factories is becoming increasingly expensive while any further expansion in these industrial areas may not be possible because of the adverse environmental effects which have yet to be brought under control. From the point of view of acquiring production resources, therefore, there seem to be clear limits to further growth of Japanese large-scale industry. The cost pressure arising from the shortage of production factors sets foreseeable limits to quantity expansion. Better quality, rationalisation of production facilities and increased productivity from the same resources are therefore gaining in importance as alternative goals.

Incentives for this also come from changes in sales or marketing conditions which have a direct bearing on profitability. In recent years Japanese management has tended to concentrate only on raising output. In the struggle for a larger share of world markets, profitability as a criterion for management decisions was often overtaken by the hope of future profit. However, the resultant excess capacities lead to threatening price recessions. Petrochemicals provide a typical example. In five years market prices have fallen by between 35% and 40% but in the the same period, when production costs were successfully reduced by up to 20%, profitability was insufficient.

This situation normally leads to rigorous export offensives which in turn disturb the international price structure and finally worsen the profit position for the companies to an even greater extent.

Excess production capacities and falling prices in large-scale industrial markets, including though to a less extent the chemical industry, indicate that the Japanese economy is entering a new phase. Above-average profits achieved in the former growth areas can only be maintained if new markets are found. This however must require some re-organisation of the major companies.

It has been repeatedly pointed out that Japanese management has enjoyed a relatively wide freedom of decision. In recent years, however, rapid economic growth has led to secondary effects which now challenge manager-ial autonomy. Particularly noteworthy is the deterioration in living conditions in the industrial areas and the in-creasing disturbance of the ecological balance of the environment.

Clearly there are limits to the encroachment of industrial development on the major Japanese economic centres and these may now have been reached. Management decisions are thus becoming the subject of public politics. A second-ary effect of industrial progress is the change in living conditions throughout Japan. The transfer of a major part of the population from the agrarian to the industrial sector and the organisation of increasingly larger groups of workers in the highly mechanised industries have led to emotional stresses. These stresses are intensified by the 'inhospitality' of Japanese cities, a characteristic not un-known in Europe.

Stability and orderly behaviour in Japanese large-scale industry must not be equated with stability and order in the total economic community. Management is inevitably becoming involved in socio-political matters which make its field of decision more complex and its actual decisions more complicated. Finally, the prospects for growth and profit-making and the social environment for business determine the freedom enjoyed by managers in their decision-making. Any changes in these prospects or con-ditions exert strong pressures for changes in management.

That companies are fully aware of this and of the

problems involved is shown by the expressed aims of the representative associations, Keizei Doyukai, Keidanren and Nikkeiren. Keizei Doyukai (Japanese Committee for Economic Development), founded in 1946 by a group of progressive businessmen, now has 1,000 members, all of whom hold top positions in industry. Its objective is to promote stable economic growth and the creation of a balanced social environment while further developing free enterprise and national welfare. It is particularly concerned with the social responsibilities of management and with the promotion of higher productivity.

Keidanren, the Federal Union of Japanese Industry, with 105 branch associations and 731 company members, strives for close relations between all branches of industry, carries out studies and enquiries into economic problems, makes representations when required to the Japanese authorities and puts forward practical proposals for solving specific industrial problems or any problems caused by industry.

Nikkeiren is the Association of Japanese Employers' Unions. Its goal is to solve industrial labour relations problems.

Kikawada Kazutaka, chairman of Keizei Doyukai, believes that the rapid economic growth in recent years has led to a serious conflict between the socio-economic system and the people. Consequently the most important problems for the next decade arise from this situation. In his view the extraordinary growth rate of the Japanese economy has also created the need for close international co-operation, particularly in the development of sources of raw materials.

This view of the problem suggests that there are several fundamental tasks, particularly the creation of a social environment in which people are able to follow a variety of pursuits of their own choice, provided they are in harmony with other people.

Kogo Uemura, of Keidanren, has written of five problems. (1) The sharp increase in wages and prices and the need to relate wage increases to productivity. This requires the co-operation of management, State and trade unions. (2) Credit restrictions which impose a nationwide competitive battle for business capital and which should be made more flexible. (3) The need for freer foreign trade and currency transfers. Further measures in this direction are strongly advocated by Keidanren. (4) Environmental pollution. Uemura points out that the fate of management in the major companies will probably depend on the correct solution to this problem. (5) State co-operation. Uemura wants effective implementation of a policy of land release and space planning, opening up of oceanic resources, improvement of Government information systems and simplification of the State fiscal administration.

At the 23rd general meeting of Nikkeiren a resolution was passed concerning 'Management Attitudes on the threshold of the 70s'. It was stated that in the final analysis the goal of economic growth is linked to human satisfaction and that industrial progress in harmony with social requirements must be the aim. There is a need for new constructive and co-operative relations between employers and employees, based on their joint social responsibility, and management must create working conditions in which people can be happy. In this connection, the significance of the industrial training and management training systems was noted.

From these opinions of representatives of Japanese management it seems there are slightly differing views on values. Uemura, for example, expresses himself quite pragmatically. He puts forward rational arguments. The statements of Keizai Doyukai are predominantly rational, as regards values. Nikkeiren's opinions are both pragmatically and morally orientated. The fluctuations between a purpose-rational and value-rational view of a problem, and the search for a synthesis, are clearly discernible in the discussions of Japanese management on the present situation and the tasks it confronts.

Heinz Hartman, in his study of the German entrepreneur, has established a similar two-tier structure of thought and argument, using the concepts of credible authority based on belief in ultimate values, and of functional authority based on material requirements. He has reached the conclusion that German entrepreneurship is characterised essentially by a value-rational attitude and that in consequence the authority relationships within an organisation are fundamentally dependent on ultimate values.

Similarly, there is a need in Japanese management to represent and to justify its interests, to present its views on problems and its strategy, on both a value-rational and a purpose-rational basis.

The problems confronting Japanese management arise from the fundamental stresses of a rapidly expanding economic community striving for security. The need for guaranteeing raw material supplies, protecting industries against international competition by tariff and other measures, binding labour to a company in order to obtain the greatest output at lowest cost, these and other measures are on quite a different level from the need for establishing partnership conditions with an open attitude to information for employees, developing a well-planned environment with an infrastructure of services meeting the needs of business and domestic life, and finally enabling all the relevant problems to be discussed and solved without acrimony.

Finally, a word on the establishment of an economic and social order which does not endanger the industrial growth of Japan and its products, from the point of view of international competition. The claim of Japanese management to take part in a joint decision-making system, with the public authorities, stems from the urgency of this problem. Of course, the limits to management autonomy are clear. The problems of growth can be solved only if the increase in productivity produces meaningful results, i.e. when industry does not harm the development of human interests. Attempts at adapting Japanese management to present-day needs must be judged in this light.

CHAPTER 18

Environmental Challenges

Management strategies in Japanese large-scale industry are needed to cover four main requirements: structural changes in the production system, market changes, industrial relations and social environment policies, and finally, relations between industry and the State.

The need for change in the production system arises from the fact that a period of growth sustained by the development of heavy engineering and the chemical industry is followed by a new period sustained by development of the consumer goods industries and by public authority investment. Since the growth of the car and television industries, like the growth of the building industry, will undoubtedly level out in the long run, the importance of new products as stimulants to industry will increase.

The ability of production systems to shift from quantity output to higher quality output must take priority in general management strategy. Numerous problems arising from changes in a large company's activities could certainly be passed on to smaller supply firms, in the predominantly dual structure of Japanese industry. Their specialisation is being advocated to an increasing degree by management in large-scale industry.

The most important feature of the changes in markets is that they have become international. Japanese large-scale industry is gradually taking on the character of multi-national companies. International trading necessarily leads to exchange activities which must be taken right to the personal level. Unlike rival companies in other countries, managements in Japan are very 'Japanese' in every respect. This cultural isolation cannot possibly be maintained.

Hence the predominant strategy is now the export of Japanese managers and management methods. The International Management Co-operation Committee arranges for experienced and skilled management experts to go to developing countries for periods of up to three months, as advisers to private enterprises. This arrangement ensures that young, very active Japanese managers acquire international experience.

Another method of exporting Japanese management techniques is offered by the Asian Productivity Organisation, whose international training programmes are organised and conducted by the Japan Productivity Centre. The Asian candidates are able to attend training courses in Japan, or they can join any one of the 10 study missions which travel to Japan every year. There are also 12-week courses for production engineers, of which 8 weeks are spent in the workshops of one of the leading companies.

Thus Japanese management is certainly making an effort to broaden the international horizon of its own nationals and at the same time give actual and prospective business partners an understanding of Japanese management techniques.

One may ask how far changes in labour organisation and social conditions will change the internal methods of Japanese management, particularly its personnel policies. There cannot yet be any question of management in large-scale industry deviating from such tried principles as permanent employment, compulsory early retirement and promotion according to seniority. These are backed by the conservative trade unions, who owe their existence to just such principles.

Thus at present management is employing compromise strategies aimed at combining the principles of efficiency and seniority in the evaluation of workers, promoting out of turn younger, qualified workers and increasing the labour potential by making the compulsory retirement system more flexible.

It is clear that while the trend is towards obtaining flexibility in personnel policy, any change that does occur will in no way be revolutionary and will not take place quickly. This is because Japanese management has always emphasised the need for harmonious internal relations, within the work force and between management and employees. The 'organisation man' in Japan should in future, as in the past, display a high degree of company loyalty.

The dependence of the development potential of large-scale industry and, therefore, of the freedom for management policies, on national planning is well known. This necessarily leads to close mutual relations between industry and the State, strengthened by the fact that many directors who came from outside the company have been in a Ministry. Managers also play an important part in advising the government.

Even if the Japanese principles of social harmony and mutual obligation, in a world dominated by business competition, seem anachronistic to Western observers, they nevertheless provide a starting point for enlisting the support of those interest groups in society who want to see the development of an economy based on co-operation. Perhaps this is why Japanese management is less exposed than Western management to the danger of isolation, as a technocratic elite, from other major social groups which have the power to limit its sphere of action.

The 30-year Japanese Miracle: Lessons for the West

by George Copeman

Japan and Germany make an interesting comparison in the opening sections of Fürstenberg's book. Indeed, it needed a German professor of sociology, specialising in the industrial environment, to make this study of the Japanese miracle, which is so like the German miracle though a little later and even more spectacular.

It would have been rather more difficult for anyone brought up in the traditions of the English-speaking world to ask the right questions. He would have been less likely to turn over so many stones with odd-looking creatures under them.

Fürstenberg has certainly shown that there are many roads to Rome, that we can too easily make unquestioned assumptions about the conditions which must, repeat 'must', be fulfilled if the business world is to prosper and grow at a satisfactory pace. We can too easily overlook the fact that in other circumstances other conditions may apply and be even more effective.

Looking at Fürstenberg's study through Anglo-Saxon eyes, and also with the eyes of an editor who has been concerned with reducing the vast amount of detail in the original German text, what are the special points about recent Japanese industrial history which stand out as contributing to the fast Japanese growth rate? I find there are 15 points:

1. The feudal Samurai tradition comes right into modern

industry and gives a special code of behaviour to the managerial and supervisory grades.

2. The history of denationalisation, selling off Government industries to the leading trading and farming families, provides a tradition of free enterprise which is not arrogant towards government but which, on the contrary, is accustomed to working with government, being assisted by it and, in turn, greatly influencing its policies.

3. The principle of permanent employment, and with it the rewarding of long service through supplements to salary and through promotion by seniority.

4. The principle of early retirement which creates vertical mobility and opportunities for advancement whilst people are young enough to give of their best.

5. The traditional system of collective decision-making which, though frequently by-passed on matters of business policy, still applies to enough areas of decision to create a feeling of participation.

6. The Government policy of cheap and plentiful capital for large-scale industry.

7. The encouragement of technical innovation in those industries which had the greatest growth potential.

8. The systematic use of a dual structure of large firms as basic material suppliers, product fabricators and market distributors, backed up by large numbers of small firms as component suppliers, the latter giving flexibility to output and removing many of the labour problems from a big firm to a small firm atmosphere.

9. Abolition of the old system of land tenure, resulting in a mass migration of new workers to industry, thus giving it an obedient and non-unionised, mobile workforce to supplement the permanent employees.

10. The use of Government subsidies to smooth out the peaks in home demand, this policy being made possible by strict control of imports, contrary to the Adam Smith doctrine of free trade so widely accepted in principle in the West.

11. Absence of Western-type trade unions, in the sense of unions confined to a particular trade, and hence an absence of over-manned jobs and inflexible operations, as so frequently found in the English-speaking world, particularly Britain. Japanese company unions have been, by comparison, rather weaker than the Anglo-Saxon trade unions.

12. The intense group-consciousness of the Japanese, which helps to restrain the friction naturally arising within any large organisation.

13. The use of large-scale marketing associations which have been able to obtain the economies and advantages of 'chain-store' types of distribution.

14. The versatility of labour arising from a general education system, on top of which is imposed company training in specialist areas, thus avoiding the demarcation troubles of the West with its traditional craft apprenticeships and its pre-determined professional and academic careers.

15. Fast individual company growth rates arising from a dynamic goal concept, based on both technical and marketing research, product development and co-operation with existing marketing and distribution channels.

At the time of writing, the Japanese miracle which has run for almost 30 years, bringing the country up to the front rank as an industrial power and producing a general standard of living on West European levels, appears to be almost ended. Future growth rates may well be similar to the general average of Western Europe or North America.

If this proves to be true, why has the miracle ended and what lessons does it provide for the West?

The causes of the ending or at least slowing-down of the miracle are inherent in some of the 15 points given to explain the fast growth. Let us pick them out:

6. *The Government policy of cheap and plentiful capital for*

large-scale industry and 7. *The encouragement of technical innovation in those industries which had the greatest growth potential.* Once a developing country has caught up with the other major industrial powers, there are no obvious areas where the application of large-scale capital can produce a certainty of great rewards. One can no longer, for example, copy the most advanced steel-making plant in the world and build it on the most economic scale. That has already been done. Everywhere one is buffeting against the frontiers of knowledge. In France and Britain, for example, it is bad enough to have to pay for Concorde. We would be foolish if we also deceived ourselves about its true cost by providing plentiful capital at cheap rates of interest.

8. *The systematic use of a dual structure of large and small firms.* No doubt the strong post-war desire for economic reconstruction, national independence and economic strength, gave a stimulus to the workings of this dual structure. However, the temptations of large companies to go on and on with the merger movement, to enhance their power through financial growth, in place of organic growth through the expansion of markets, is likely to disrupt the Japanese dual structure, as it has in the West. One of the nearest Western equivalents to the Japanese dual structure is the relationship between Marks and Spencer Ltd. and their suppliers. One of the strengths of M and S is that they do not buy up their suppliers. But can the Japanese giants resist this temptation?

9. *Abolition of the old system of land tenure, resulting in a mass migration of new workers to industry, thus giving it an obedient and non-unionised, mobile work force to supplement the permanent employees.* This is a once-for-all gain, the effects of which wear off as the new recruits to industry become more sophisticated, more conscious of their new labouring and non-owning status. It is part of a world-wide historic process. Look at these facts:

1. The British Industrial Revolution was preceded by an Agricultural Revolution, when people came off the land into the towns.

2. Nineteenth century America absorbed millions of European immigrants and grew very fast.

3. The German Economic Miracle of the 1950s and 1960s was fed firstly by migrating East Germans and later by Turks and Yugoslavs.

4. The French fast growth rate seems to owe much to a ready supply of pieds-noirs, as well as to the peasant farmers who came down out of the hills.

5. The fast rate of South African economic growth can be largely explained by the migration of Bantu to the towns.

6. The Japanese miracle has been continually fed by a supply of peasant labour off the farms.

To Westerners the figures on Japan are scarcely believable, but it is worth repeating that between 1956 and 1961 the Japanese gross national product doubled and thereafter throughout the 1960s it continued growing by over 11% per annum. Side by side with this, however, we must put the fact that as recently as 1955, 40·5% of all Japanese workers were still engaged in agriculture. Only 14 years later this proportion had fallen to 18·8%—representing a migration of millions of people to the towns.

Such an enormous flow of raw recruits to industry would have a disciplinary effect. When they arrived and for years afterwards, the new recruits would be on their best behaviour, unorganised, undemanding and fearful as individuals of putting a foot wrong in their new environment. Moreover, their very arrival would create promotion opportunities for the older hands. Everyone promotable who had any length of seniority would be likely to receive his chance. Problems of industrial relations would be minimised by this climate.

Democracy in the ancient Greek city state was based on slavery. Now that slavery is officially abolished, it would seem that the modern alternative, if you want trouble-free industrial relations, is to get yourself a continuing supply of naïve peasants.

If you cannot get enough peasants, or if you don't happen to like this sort of approach to human life, there is another way. This is to treat people with dignity, perhaps even take them in as shareholders in the business and make an effort to win their full co-operation. There may be no miracles, but on the evidence available, substantially higher growth rates may be achieved.

10. *The use of Government subsidies to smooth out the peaks in home demand, this policy being made possible by strict control of imports, contrary to the Adam Smith doctrine of free trade so widely accepted in principle in the West.* Here again, this policy becomes more and more difficult to sustain as the standard of living of the Japanese people rises and their purchases become more sophisticated. Inevitably other countries want to come closer to a balance of trade with Japan. This means permitting the import of more and more consumer goods from abroad, which the Japanese people have become accustomed to having. Hence it becomes more and more difficult to impose sudden, arbitrary restrictions on imports. Unless this can be done, however, as the British know particularly well, it becomes extremely difficult to subsidise home demand without running into a balance of payments crisis.

12. *The intense group-consciousness of the Japanese, which helps to restrain the friction naturally arising within any large organisation.* As time goes by this is likely to work against Japanese fast growth, when more and more employees realise that they are a separate group from the owners of the business and that their identity of interest lies more with fellow employees than with the company as a whole, including its shareholders. A remarkable feature of Fürstenberg's book is that it scarcely mentions ownership.

In this respect the book belongs to the Peter Drucker school of thought, which regards management as an art or science involving the use of people and other resources in order to satisfy customers and obtain black figures on the bottom line, without any particular concern as to who owns the capital and hence who gets the benefit of the black figures, or bears the loss if they are red.

Anyone running his own business usually regards this neglect of the importance of ownership as nonsense. If you ask him to sign away his share capital on condition that he can stay to manage the business, he will tell you to go to hell. Ownership is important to him, as indeed it is to any house-owner.

Though I am a great admirer of Drucker and his contribution to management know-how, I regard as misleading the notion that large-scale company management can be a professional practice divorced from the question of ownership. In my experience, some of the biggest problems of large public companies and of nationalised industries arise from the separation of ownership and control. The workers, including the top management workers, are present, but the owners are absent. In these circumstances any kind of permanent group-consciousness embracing the whole enterprise is impossible.

Japan is heading for as much trouble from this quarter as are the Western industrial democracies. Trouble will be delayed only by the continued existence, if this is possible, of a dual system in Japan, one arm of which contains a very large number of family firms in which ownership and control are closely identified. This, however, is only a delaying factor. The big company problem, where ownership is largely divorced from control, needs to be tackled, in my view, by the extension of direct employee share ownership.

Having looked at the temporary factors which suggest

an early end to the Japanese miracle of high growth rate, we can now turn to study the factors which are likely to go on sustaining the miracle. This may suggest similar factors or circumstances in the West, from which lessons may be learnt about how to create the conditions for sustained economic growth.

1. *The feudal Samurai tradition comes right into modern industry and gives a special code of behaviour to the managerial and supervisory grades.* This Samurai tradition may be compared with three Western traditions: Firstly, the British public school esprit de corps. This derives from teenage boys being given a particular type of education and at the same time learning to rub off on each other by living together and playing team games. It provides an undoubtedly useful basis of mutual trust, but it can be divisive if only a very limited number of potential leaders of industry can acquire this particular background.

Secondly, the Prussian military and civil service tradition. The main contribution here comes from thoroughness and attention to detail, which are great assets when combined with versatility, though they are potential liabilities if they lead to unthinking obedience and routine.

Thirdly, the North English and Scottish non-conformist small business tradition, or as it became known in America, the Protestant Ethic. Here is the real core of self-reliant entrepreneurship, owning and running an independent business, paying creditors on time and keeping free from excessive reliance on the banks, treating a man's word as his bond, having special regard for employees, particularly long service ones, and beholden to no man save the customer, who is king.

American business literature has thoroughly discussed 'the decline of the Protestant Ethic', and this decline has been largely attributed to the rise of the giant corporation, where every manager is Mr. Facing Both Ways, where internal politics sometimes overshadow the day-to-day necessity of satisfying customers, and where every man's job is in jeopardy for reasons which may or may not have anything to do with his economic performance.

The restoration of this ethic seems to depend on two factors: firstly, the organisation of large businesses into as many natural unit businesses or profit centres as possible, and secondly, the spreading of share ownership amongst employees, particularly the managers and long-service employees, so that the circumstances of the independent entrepreneur are reproduced as closely as possible.

2. *The history of denationalisation . . . provides a tradition of free enterprise which is not arrogant towards government but which, on the contrary, is accustomed to working with government.* France provides the best Western example of Government-business co-operation in the style of the Japanese. France is aided in this by the fact that her most prestigious institutions of learning, such as the Ecole Polytechnique, concentrate rather less on history and the classical languages than do their nearest equivalents among the Anglo-Saxons, and they concentrate rather more on mathematics, science and engineering. To be an engineer in France means to enjoy more prestige than in the English-speaking world.

Moreover, the top levels of the civil service in any country tend to be recruited from the most prestigious places of learning. It therefore follows that in France the top civil servants find it easier to talk the same language as the men who run, or at least who plan the big business operations. So to design a French five-year plan which actually assists the business world and makes it grow is not overly difficult.

As for denationalisation, the French have not done this, though they have recognised the need for enabling employees in nationalised firms such as Renault to feel a sense of participation, a sharing in the ownership of the business.

Under a special law introduced in December, 1969,

provision was made for Renault employees to be issued
with shares in the company, and this same measure has
since been extended to the nationalised banks and in-
surance companies.

Let us look at how the system works in Renault. The
maximum eventual shareholding of the employees is
limited to 25% of the total capital of the company, in
order that Renault may 'retain its national character'.

Entitlement to participate is based on length of service
and level of responsibility, with a minimum requirement
of five years' service. Shares are issued without payment,
and no tax is charged on this 'notional income' either at
the time of issue or at the time of subsequent sale. There
is no capital gains tax in France. Shares may not be sold
for five years, and then only to other employees or to a
special company-administered fund which has the responsibility of regulating an internal market in the shares.

3. *The principle of permanent employment, and with it the
rewarding of long service through supplements to salary and through
promotion by seniority.* The nearest Western equivalent to this
was in the air forces during the Second World War, when
a flyer who lived long enough was automatically promoted
through the junior officer grades and in some cases into the
beginings of senior officer rank. These were, however,
exceptional circumstances. Permanent employment and
automatic rises in pay, but not automatic promotion, are
associated with the Civil Service in Western countries, not
with the business world.

There is, however, a German contribution in this area,
coming from J. H. Von Thünen, a nineteenth-century
economist. He recognised that there is a case for employees
with some length of service having a residual right to part
of the continuing income of an organisation to which they
have contributed labour over a period of years. In practice,
a right to residual income is most conveniently and neatly
expressed in the form of ownership of shares.

From the work of Von Thünen comes the typical American deferred profit-sharing plan, of which there are now over 150,000 in operation in U.S. companies. Many of these plans weight their company contributions in favour of the long-service employee, both to encourage long service and more particularly to encourage participation in the scheme by long-service employees. This means that the real opinion-formers in the company, the long service people, who set the attitudes and the level of morale, virtually all become shareholders in the company. During their later years they become very significant shareholders. Thus their attitudes tend to reflect a harmonious relationship between labour and capital.

Most famous of these 150,000 company schemes is that of Sears Roebuck, the largest retail group in the world. In 1972 the 78 employees who retired with 40 or more years' service received an average payout of $438,170. Of this sum, their average contribution during all the years they had been in the scheme was only $9,686, so the vast bulk of the funds they received were company contributions invested in common stock which had grown in value over the years, together with reinvested dividend income. As the employee's contribution to this scheme is 5% of pay with a minimum annual contribution of $750 (formerly $500), the scheme is certainly not favourable to the higher-paid. This makes its results even more spectacular for average-paid employees.

Briefly, the scheme works like this. Employees with at least 12 months' service may contribute 5% of their annual pay and the company matches this contribution, on a rising scale, as follows:

up to 5 years' service—once times the employee's contribution.
5 to 10 years' service—twice the employee's contribution.

over 10 years' service—three times the employee's contribution.

over 15 years' service
and over 50 years of age—four times the employee's contribution.

All but about 15% of the total funds held by trustees on behalf of participants in the scheme are invested in Sears common stock. The balance is invested in about 80 'blue chip' listed companies and broadly represents the employees' own contributions. Thus, if through some freak occurrence the company had to close down, provided that these other investments were still good, employees could at least receive their own contributions back.

After five years, each annual contribution by the company vests in the employee, so that if he leaves the company's service before retirement or death, he receives not only his own contributions but also those vested. On normal retirement or death, or course, he receives the benefit of all his own contributions and all those made by the company for him.

4. *The principle of early retirement which creates vertical mobility and opportunities for advancement whilst people are young enough to give of their best.* Retirement ages in the West are coming down but are still 10 to 15 years ahead of the Japanese levels. The acceptance of early retirement is made easier for the Japanese by the widespread practice of re-engaging the retired person the day he retires, for another position elsewhere in the company, though with reduced status. Even so, the economic circumstances of early retired persons in Japan are frequently rather tight.

One way for the West to make early retirement more palatable would be through the widespread adoption of deferred profit-sharing schemes. These would provide employees with the prospect that, if they worked together and made the business successful, they could have significant extra funds accumulated for early retirement.

Sears Roebuck figures provide an example. The average employee retiring from the company in 1972 took with him $90,000 of stock. By contrast, as already mentioned, those with 40 or more years of service took an average of $438,170. Is it surprising that many employees decided to retire early, and that as a result mainly of early retirement, the percentage of Sears stock held by current employees fell from 24·9% in 1963 to 19·6% in 1972. A further percentage of stock would, of course, be held by former employees, now retired.

There is a sequence of events here. Company success makes it possible for employees to retire early, but early retirements create promotion opportunities for younger people, they create vertical job mobility and help to keep a company continually rejuvenated. Hence it has an enhanced prospect of continuing success. So the system of early retirement is automatically financed by company achievements.

5. *The traditional system of collective decision-making . . . still applies to enough areas of decision to create a feeling of participation.* In the West the most highly developed system of participation is in Germany, where there is employee representation on the supervisory boards of the larger companies and also a system of works councils giving employees, through their elected representatives, very considerable rights of consultation and even, in some cases, of veto over their terms and conditions of work.

This may well be fine, but it carries with it the danger of further separating ownership from control.

Whenever I hear of proposals for employee participation in management decisions without parallel proposals for employee participation in share ownership, I feel sad. If employees take on some of the responsibilities of management without also participating in the potential capital rewards, this in my view is a poor deal. And like all poor deals, it must in due course lead to trouble. If the present body of shareholders surrender some of the responsibilities of management whilst retaining all the after-tax rewards, they will sooner or later come to be regarded by most people as a redundant group, ripe for expropriation. Private ownership will thus drastically diminish and with it the prospects of ensuring personal initiative in the development of new products and services, to satisfy new customer demands and sustain rising prosperity.

11. *Absence of Western-type trade unions.* . . . The story of the Japanese miracle rise in living standards suggests, as does the German miracle, that the chief millstone around the necks of Western workers, preventing them from gaining higher standards of living, may well be their trade unions. It is not so much the fact of having a union as the way it is organised, which makes or mars the prospect of rising living standards.

The science of economics is not yet exact enough for us to know whether Japanese inflation of the mid-70s, running at 20% per annum, coupled with union demands at the time of writing of 30% per annum, is on balance a good thing or a bad. Is the beneficial effect of raising home demand greater or less than the effect on export market costs and on investment decisions?

The answer depends on a number of factors and is arguable, but what we know for certain is that the type of craft trade union restrictions which exist in Britain, the pioneer of the industrial revolution and hence of trade unionism, is definitely harmful to the growth of living standards.

Any country such as Germany which can start again in the late 1940s with just 16 unions organised on an industrial, not a craft basis, or any country such as Japan which can begin with company or house unions, is at a definite advantage. The steadily increasing federation of company unions in Japan, on a national basis, obviously increases overall union bargaining power and it remains to be seen what the net effect of this will be, but there is certainly a permanent gain from not having unnecessary restrictions and demarcation disputes.

It will be obvious that any extension of employee share ownership in the coming years, which enables employees to identify more closely with the company where they work, is an aid to breaking down restrictive barriers between working groups.

13. *The uses of large-scale marketing associations which have been able to obtain the economies and advantages of 'chain-store' types of distribution.* There is probably not a lot which is new in Japanese marketing which is not known to the leading chains in the English-speaking world. Nevertheless, the Japanese achievements underline the contribution to economic progress which efficient marketing is making or can make in many countries.

14. *The versatility of labour arising from a general education system, on top of which is imposed company training in specialist areas, thus avoiding the demarcation troubles of the West with its traditional craft apprenticeships and its pre-determined professional and academic careers.* In the West, the development of computers and their application to many different tasks in business, provide the supreme example of company training given to people whose original education was quite general, or was at least remote from the technology of computers.

When computers were first being installed, in the early 1950s, it was thought that the staff recruited to run them should have honours degrees in mathematics. Within a year or two, ordinary degrees in any subject were regarded as adequate qualification. A few years later it was realised that no degree at all was necessary. Early in the 1960s, aptitude tests came into widespread use which distinguished fairly accurately between those people who were suitable for systems analysis or programming on computers, and those who were not. It was then found that the people who passed the tests and proved to be good at this work had no common factors in their educational background. Some had done poorly at school and had had no further education. Some had taken good degrees. Moreover, the range of subjects studied, at school or later, varied widely.

Previous education and training have thus been found to be largely irrelevant to computer work. The company can, either internally or externally, provide the specific education and training needed. This system allows for much greater flexibility in meeting changing needs, than when reliance is placed on qualifications previously gained in the public, state-run education system.

Salesmanship is another major area of modern skills where nearly all the training, in the Western world, is provided by the employing company and relatively little is provided by the state-run education system. Together, salesmanship and computers now occupy a substantial slice of all business employment and this is a growing slice. Technological subjects in the West are, by contrast, dominated by the State-run education system. It is in this area that there is less flexibility and more demarcation.

15. *Fast individual company growth rates arising from a dynamic goal concept, based on both technical and marketing research, product development and co-operation with existing marketing and distribution channels.* This description of entrepreneurship is usually associated with small enterprises, not large. The small enterprise will not necessarily, however, be independent. It may be part of a larger group. Indeed, it may need the management resources, such as market research, of a large organisation, as well as its capital resources and its distribution channels.

For maximum prospect of economic growth, a dual system of large and small companies seems to be needed. Sometimes the entrepreneur-type manager develops his skills in a large organisation and then hives off into his own business. Sometimes he starts in his own business and later sells part of his shareholding to a large organisation so that he has the backing of its capital and other resources.

Either way, a necessary condition is a public policy for the continual spreading of capital ownership throughout the population. Such a policy would aim to maximise the chance that a budding entrepreneur will find capital available to start up his business, either from his own purse or from those of his family or friends.

The absence of any study of capital ownership is a major omission from Fürstenberg's book, for this subject is the Achilles heel of the Japanese miracle. The same, however, may be said about Western countries and their prospects of continuing economic growth. This subject needs rather more attention than it is normally given in the arena of public policy.

Index